Japanese Criminal Justice

Japanese Criminal Justice

A. Didrick Castberg

PRAEGER

New York
Westport, Connecticut
London

Library of Congress Cataloging-in-Publication Data

Castberg, A. Didrick.
    Japanese criminal justice / A. Didrick Castberg.
        p.   cm.
    Includes bibliographical references.
    ISBN 0-275-93355-5 (alk. paper)
    1. Criminal justice, Administration of—Japan.   I. Title.
    HV9960.J3C37   1990
    364.952—dc20   90-32792

British Library Cataloguing in Publication Data is available.

Library of Congress Catalog Card Number: 90-32792
ISBN: 0-275-93355-5

First published in 1990

Praeger Publishers, One Madison Avenue, New York, NY 10010
An imprint of Greenwood Publishing Group, Inc.

Printed in the United States of America

The paper used in this book complies with the
Permanent Paper Standard issued by the National
Information Standards Organization (Z39.48-1984).

10 9 8 7 6 5 4 3 2 1

Contents

Illustrations

Preface

Japan is a fascinating country. It is the subject of books and articles, motion pictures, and television news programs and specials. Interest in Japan is reflected in the small but dedicated following that sumo, a most Japanese sport, is attracting in the United States and Great Britain. Japan is part of the mystical East, with a culture that is at once similar yet vastly different from our own. I am amazed that a country that was devastated by war can so quickly emerge as an economic giant, that "made in Japan" can denote high quality only decades after it meant shoddiness. I am further perplexed over how a country can change so much and yet retain so many traditions and values, how highly selective the country is about what aspects of foreign influence it will adopt, and how people can live in such close proximity to each other in its major cities and enjoy a crime rate that is many times lower than that of other industrialized nations. Japan is a land of contradictions, and that is what makes it so fascinating.

My fascination with Japan and things Japanese has led to a curiosity about the country and to the inevitable question: What can we learn from Japan? The problems that affect us the most but that the Japanese seem to have solved are those that attract the most initial attention. A good deal of attention has been paid to the economic successes of Japan and to how Japanese management and production techniques might be applied to the United States, but as the Japanese economy slows and the United States economy picks up, attention shifts to other areas of concern, such as crime. What explains the very low crime rate in Japan? Why is the crime rate in urban areas of Japan lower than in rural areas, reversing the pattern found in most other countries? Why is their drug problem so insignificant compared to ours? If we can find answers to these questions, we might be able to solve some of our own problems. Unfortunately, there is little literature to which we can turn. There are few books on the subject of crime and criminal justice in Japan, and the articles that exist, many of which are quite good, are so scattered among law reviews, comparative law journals, and interdisciplinary scholarly journals that it is quite difficult to obtain an overall view of the Japanese system. This book hopes to rectify that situation.

Comparative research is fraught with dangers. Cultural biases hinder objectivity, unfamiliarity with a culture often results in misunderstandings and misinterpretations, and language differences impede research. And yet, such research must take place if we are to understand the processes of other nations and if we expect to solve some of our own problems. If we truly do live in a world community, with common problems that can only be solved through mutual understanding and cooperation, we must forge ahead in comparative research, aware of the difficulties inherent in such research but undaunted nevertheless.

I conducted the research that resulted in this book during a 1987-88 Fulbright lectureship and sabbatical in Japan. I am not a Japan specialist. I had an interest in Japan, partially as a result of a general fascination with the mysterious East and partially as a result of living closer to Japan than most other Americans; Hawaii has been significantly affected by Japanese culture for the past century. The primary intent of the Fulbright lectureship was to teach Japanese college students about the United States Constitution and constitutional system during the bicentennial of the Constitution. Because research is not a major part of a Fulbright lectureship (there are separate Fulbright research awards), my initial intent was to conduct a preliminary study of Japanese police-prosecutor relations during time away from the classroom and speaking obligations. The bulk of the research took place after completing the Fulbright lectureship period during the sabbatical. During the preliminary phases of the research it became clear that very little in English had been written about the Japanese criminal justice system in general, although specific aspects of it had been covered quite well. The scope of the project was then expanded to cover the entire system.

I speak very little Japanese, despite having taken courses in the subject. My ability in the language was sufficient to conduct simple daily transactions but not to conduct interviews or read scholarly works in the language; thus, I had to rely on English-speaking interviewees or translators. To what extent this adversely affected my research is not known, but it was bound to have some effect. Nevertheless, my findings are for the most part consistent with the findings of Japanese-speaking scholars whose native language is English, as well as with the translated works of

Japanese scholars. I believe I am sensitive to the Japanese culture, having experienced a good deal of it while living in Hawaii for over twenty-five years. I ate raw fish (*sashimi*) and took off my shoes before entering a home for decades before living in Japan, so I experienced no culture shock upon arrival or while living in Japan. On the other hand, I had not studied Japanese culture, let alone Japanese criminal justice, prior to 1987. Nor was I particularly experienced in cross-cultural research. There was, then, a lot to learn in a relatively short period of time. Let the reader be the judge of the success of the research project.

Many people contributed to this project in a variety of ways. The Council for the International Exchange of Scholars (Fulbright) program and its Japanese arm, the Japan–United States Educational Commission (JUSEC), provided for my travel to Japan, institutional affiliations, and numerous other assistance, without which none of this would have been possible. Carolyn Matano Yang and her staff at JUSEC were outstanding. The faculties of British and American Studies and of Law at Nanzan University and the Law faculty at Nagoya University provided expertise, encouragement, and companionship for over a year. Although I hesitate to single people out for fear of missing somebody, I do want to especially thank the following individuals: Professors Fukuji Taguchi and Yasutomo Morigiwa of the Nagoya University Law faculty; Professor Ichiro Iwano, Director of the Center for American Studies at Nanzan University; Professors Yoshio Hagino and Shugo Minagawa of the Nanzan Law faculty; Professor Roger Hashizume of the Law faculty at Chukyo University; and the "Common Room Gang" at Nanzan—Mark, Dave, Scott, Kotaro—who provided not only assistance but needed levity. Unfortunately, the police officials, prosecutors, defense attorneys, and judges who so graciously agreed to be interviewed—some many times—must remain anonymous, as I would not want my interpretations to be taken as official statements by these very helpful and gracious professionals. I would be remiss, however, if I did not single out one of these professionals—"T.A."—who not only provided a great deal of information about the Japanese criminal justice system but also had the patience to keep answering my stupid questions. My colleagues at the University of Hawaii at Hilo, Professors Lawrence Rogers, Richard Howell, and Masafumi Honda, endured many questions dealing with translations of Japanese terms and provided needed help and advice. Finally, my wife, Joan Eguchi Castberg, suffered the pitfalls of a Japanese-American in Japan while supporting, prodding, encouraging, and intellectually stimulating me. To them all: *Dōmo arigatō gozaimashita.*

1

Crime and Criminal Justice in Japan: An Overview

The Japanese legal system in general, and its criminal justice component in particular, seems at first glance to be very similar to its counterpart in the United States. The institutions seem to be much like those in the United States, while the penal code and the code of criminal procedure often seem to be almost word-for-word equivalents of United States codes. The provisions of the Japanese Constitution dealing with criminal procedure are also often identical to the United States Bill of Rights. As we shall see, there are very good reasons for these seeming similarities—a good deal of the Japanese code and constitutional material dealing with criminal justice was written by Americans. As is often the case in Japan, however, what seems on the surface to be one thing is often something else entirely.

Japanese law was not always influenced by foreign law, of course. Early Japanese law was based largely on religion, with little differentiation between secular and nonsecular rules and norms and no separate procedures or institutions to deal with the few offenses that might have been called criminal (Noda 1976: 20-22). Beginning in the seventh century, however, Japanese law rapidly came under the influence of Chinese law, which was based on Confucian ideals. This law was characterized by distinct criminal codes and rules of procedure, with criminal proceedings being instituted initially by the victim or by any citizen and later by government officials. Although criminal procedure at the time was unsophisticated by current standards, it did feature aspects of the adversary process as well as an appeal procedure;

it also allowed torture as a means of extracting a confession as well as compensation based only on suspicion that a crime was committed (Dando 1965: 12-13). During this same period of time specialized legal study was established at the national level, resulting in a group of legal scholars who produced a large number of official commentaries (Noda 1976: 24). The Chinese influence soon waned, with the law taking on a more distinctly Japanese nature and the Confucian influence being replaced with a secular, imperial order, characterized by fewer procedural safeguards for the accused (Noda 1976: 25).

Criminal codes gradually fell into disuse during the later stages of the Heian period (794-1185), with precedent based on rulings by the Office of Police and Judiciary becoming dominant (Dando 1965: 13). The rise of the military and resultant weakening of the central government brought about the codes of feudal militarism that lasted well into the nineteenth century (Noda 1976: 26). This period saw a great deal of internal violence in the struggles between regional *daimyo* (lords) until 1603 when Tokugawa Ieyasu was able to unify the country under a single feudal regime. The Tokugawa period lasted until 1868, when imperial power was restored under the Emperor Meiji (Noda 1976: 31-32; Dando 1965:13-14). In 1853 Commodore Matthew Perry, U.S.N., had delivered a letter from President Fillmore to the Emperor politely requesting Japan to end its isolation and open its doors to trade with the West, and this event set the stage for significant foreign influence on the institutions of Japan. The effect on the legal system was a move to greater modernization and the development of laws that would facilitate increased trade with the West.

The French Napoleonic codes proved as attractive to the Japanese as they had to other modernizing nations, and they were soon translated into Japanese. Although not fully adopted by the Japanese, their influence was significant. This influence found its way into the criminal law and procedure through the efforts of Gustave Emile Boissonade de Fortarabie, a French legal scholar, who was asked by the Japanese government to draft a penal code and a code of criminal procedure. He completed this task in 1877, and the codes were translated into Japanese, approved by the legislature, and finnally adopted in 1880. They took effect in 1882. (Takayanagi 1963: 163 Noda 1976: 45.) The Penal Code (*Keihō*) of 1880 was notable for its establishment in Japan of the principles of *nullum crimen, nulla poena sine lege* (no crime, no punishment without law) and prohibition of the use of *ex post facto* laws, equality before the law, and the concept of personal (as opposed to collective or associative) guilt. The Penal Code of 1880 was in effect for twenty-five years (Takayanagi: 165-66).

Gustave Boissonade's Penal Code was accompanied by a Code of Criminal Instruction (*Chizai Hō*), which adopted the inquisitorial method common to France and much of the rest of Europe at the time. This system made use of a preliminary investigation (*yoshin*) that was designed to determine the facts of the case prior to trial. Nonadversarial in nature, it gave great discretion to the judge in questioning the accused and any witnesses that could provide relevant information, and while it preserved the legal presumption of innocence, it resulted in a de facto presumption of guilt (ibid.: 169-70). The trial itself relied heavily on the results of the preliminary investigation. Although Boissonade provided for a jury system in his code, the feature was not adopted by the legislature.

During this twenty-five year period, German law was progressively becoming more influential in Japan, in part due to the large numbers of Japanese who studied in Germany and in part due to the very nature of German law which appealed to the Japanese. This German influence resulted in the Penal Code of 1907, a substantial revision of the 1880 code. The new code was shorter, provided greater judicial discretion in sentencing, and eliminated the principle of *nullum crimen, nulla poena sine lege*, a protection still found, however, in the Meiji Constitution (ibid.: 166-67). Although minor revisions have been made to the code over the years, it remains substantially unchanged today. This code will be discussed in more detail below.

Just as German law influenced the Penal Code, so, too, it influenced criminal procedure. Thus the Code of Criminal Procedure (*Keiji Soshō Hō*) of 1922 was based to a large extent on German codes and gave greater protection to the accused. Several years later, the Jury Act (*Baishin Hō*) was passed. This law, which became effective in 1928, provided for a jury that did not determine guilt but answered questions of fact put to it by the court. The jury operated on the basis of majority rule rather than unanimity and was advisory only—its answers were not binding on the court. The jury never gained much popularity in Japan, most trials were jury-waived, and the law was suspended during World War II and never reinstituted (ibid.: 171-72).

Part of the process of modernization in Japan was the writing of a constitution, and here, too, German influence was felt. Both Japanese scholars who had studied German constitutional law and German scholars played a role in drafting a constitution in the 1880s. The final product was promulgated by the emperor in 1889 (Noda 1976: 55-56). As might be expected, the constitution provided substantial powers for the emperor, with the Diet being only a consultative body, and had no bill of rights and few other provisions protecting the rights of criminal defendants.

THE POST-WAR ERA

The occupation of Japan by United States forces brought about substantial changes in legal institutions. The constitution of 1889 was thrown out and a new one written, with the primary purpose being to demilitarize and fully democratize Japan. The emperor became a figurehead and the Diet a true parliamentary body. The judiciary became independent and the new document contained many provisions similar to the United States Constitution's Bill of Rights. One could well argue, in fact, that the Japanese Constitution of 1947 contains greater protections for the accused than the United States Constitution. Specific provisions regarding criminal procedure are as follows:

Article 32. No person shall be denied the right of access to the courts.

Article 33. No person shall be apprehended except upon warrant issued by a competent judicial officer that specifies the offense with which the person is charged, unless he is apprehended while the offense is being committed.

Article 34. No person shall be arrested or detained without being at once informed of the charges against him or without the immediate privilege of counsel; nor shall he be detained without adequate cause; and upon demand of any person such cause must be immediately shown in open court in his presence and the presence of his counsel.

Article 35. The right of all persons to be secure in their homes, papers, and effects against entries, searches, and seizures shall not be impaired except upon warrant issued for adequate cause and particularly describing the place to be searched and things to be seized, or except as provided by Article 33.

(2) Each search or seizure shall be made upon separate warrant issued by a competent judicial officer.

Article 36. The infliction of torture by any public officer and cruel punishments are absolutely forbidden.

Article 37. In all criminal cases the accused shall enjoy the right to a speedy and public trial by an impartial tribunal.

(2) He shall be permitted full opportunity to examine all witnesses, and he shall have the right of compulsory process for obtaining witnesses on his behalf at public expense.

(3) At all times the accused shall have the assistance of competent counsel who shall, if the accused is unable to secure the same by his own efforts, be assigned to his use by the State.

Article 38. No person shall be compelled to testify against himself.

(2) Confession made under compulsion, torture or threat, or after prolonged arrest or detention shall not be admitted in evidence.

(3) No person shall be convicted or punished in cases where the only proof against him is his own confession

Article 39. No person shall be held criminally liable for an act that was lawful at the time it was committed, or of which he has been acquitted, nor shall he be placed in double jeopardy.

Article 40. Any person, in case he is acquitted after he has been arrested or detained, may sue the State for redress as provided by law.

A brief examination of the provisions above will reveal that they provide greater protection for the accused than does the United States Bill of Rights. The Bill of Rights has, of course, been extensively interpreted by the United States Supreme Court for almost two hundred years, and as a result the accused in the United States enjoy many protections not explicitly provided for in the first eight amendments. And as we shall see, not all provisions of the Japanese Constitution as cited above are interpreted as literally as might be expected, nor are many of the provisions rigorously enforced. The criminal procedure provisions of the Japanese Constitution are nevertheless remarkable for their farsightedness and liberalism.

Some have argued that the new constitution was imposed on the Japanese people, but as is often the case, the truth is more complex. General Douglas MacArthur, the Supreme Commander for the Allied Powers (SCAP), had few instructions from Washington with regard to a constitution for Japan, and therefore took it upon himself to not only introduce democracy to Japan but to play a major role in the writing of the new constitution (Manchester 1978: 586-878). After initially giving the task of rewriting the Meiji Constitution to Baron Kijūrō Shidehara, the new prime minister, and having that effort bog down in clashes between liberals and conservatives on the committee appointed by Shidehara, MacArthur himself wrote key sections of the document. This new constitution was then submitted to the cabinet and to the Diet for their consideration (an act that was primarily symbolic in nature), and subsequently approved. The constitution received the support of Emperor Hirohito (now Emperor Showa), which guaranteed support by the vast majority of the citizens of Japan. MacArthur called it "probably the single most important accomplishment of the occupation, for it brought to the Japanese people freedoms and privileges which they had never known" (ibid.: 590).

A new code of criminal procedure was required in order to implement the provisions of the new constitution, and accordingly such a code was written in the spring of 1948. The code was hammered out by a group of Japanese legal scholars and Allied officials over a period of several months, and the final document was approved by the Diet in 1949 without change (Oppler 1977: 13-15). It clearly reflects the Anglo-American legal tradition, eliminating the preliminary investigation and making the procedure accusatorial rather than inquisitorial, establishing an independent judiciary, and separating the prosecutors from the judiciary where they had been organizationally situated under the old code.[1] The code contains seven books. Book I, with sixteen chapters, deals with general provisions, such as jurisdiction, documents, evidence, and witnesses. Book II has three chapters dealing with inquiry and investigation, public action, and public trial. Book III deals with appeal in four chapters, while the remaining books deal with the following topics without separate chapters: reopening of procedure (IV), extraordinary appeal (V), summary procedure (VI), and execution of decision (VII).

THE LEGAL FRAMEWORK

Japan is a civil law nation, unlike the United States, which retains its common law heritage from England. As such, "the law" in Japan is found

almost exclusively in its five codes: civil, commercial, penal, criminal procedure, and civil procedure. Appellate court decisions, while having some
precedential value, do not play the role that they do in the United States or
other common law countries. It is to the codes that lawyers and judges first
look for answers to legal questions in Japan, and only after that would they
turn to appellate court decisions. The primary role that these decisions play
is in the interpretation or construction of provisions of the codes (Tanaka
1976: 61). According to Article 4 of the Courts Law (*Saibansho Hō*), a decision by an appellate court is binding on lower courts only with respect to
that particular case, and not with respect to other cases that raise the same
issue. Lower courts will, however, give great deference to higher courts, so
while they are not legally bound to follow precedent, they often do. This is
especially true in cases where the full court of fifteen justices sits (only for
the most important cases) or where the court overturns a previous decision.
Japanese appellate courts, then, are in a position to make policy through
such interpretations, although not to the extent that such policy is made in
the United States. Another significant difference between the two systems is
found in the extent to which appellate courts in each country refer to the
legislative history of a statute as a basis for interpreting that statute. While
this is a common occurrence in the United States, it is relatively rare in
Japan. Scholarly articles, on the other hand, tend to be more influential on
courts in Japan (ibid.: 97-98).

It should be understood that while precedent in Japan does not play the
role that it does in the United States, it is still quite important from a practical point of view, for it is the best way to predict how a court will interpret
a particular statute. The issue of just what role the appellate court plays in
Japan has been the subject of much scholarly debate, a debate that is still
not resolved (see Tanaka 1976: 143-62, and Beer 1984: 20-21).

As one might expect in a civil law system, the codes are quite extensive.
The Penal Code consists of 264 articles, and this code does not cover all
criminal acts. There is the Minor Offenses Law (*Keihanzai Hō*), the
Stimulant Control Law (*Kakuseizai Torishimari Hō*), the Narcotic Control
Law (*Mayaku Torishimari Hō*), the Opium Law (*Ahen Hō*), the Cannabis
Control Law (*Taima Torishimari Hō*), the Poisonous and Deleterious
Substances Control Law (*Dokubutsu Oyobi Gekibutsu Torishimari Hō*),
the Firearms and Swords Law (*Jūhō Tōkenrui Tō Shoji Torishimari Hō*),
and many other such laws dealing with specific categories of offenses not in-
cluded in the Penal Code. Even traffic offenses are considered crimes in
Japan and are classified into two categories: traffic professional negligence
(*Kōtsū Kankei Gyō Kashitsu*) (when a death or serious injury is involved)
and simple road-traffic violations, which are covered by the Road Traffic
Law (*Dōro Kōtsū Hō*) and by regulations under that law promulgated by the
cabinet.[2] The new code was the product of the Legislative Investigation
Committee, appointed by the Japanese government and consisting of
leading legal scholars, judges, prosecutors, and Ministry of Justice officials,

and representatives of the Allied occupation powers (Meyers 1977: 69). The actual offenses found in the Penal Code and specialized laws read much the same as offenses in other countries. Article 236 of the Penal Code, for example, reads as follows:

A person who deprives another of the property through violence or intimidation thereby commits the crime of robbery and shall be punished with imprisonment at forced labor for a limited term of not less than five years.

Note that the definition of the offense of robbery is much more concise than that normally found in United States statutes. Nor does the Japanese code distinguish among degrees of robbery (there is no distinction between felonies and misdemeanors in the code). Finally, terms are not defined in the code. Section 708-860 of the Hawaii Penal Code is typical of United States robbery statutes:

(1) A person commits the offense of robbery in the first degree if, in the course of committing theft:
    (a) He attempts to kill another, or intentionally inflicts or attempts to inflict grave bodily injury upon another; or
    (b) He is armed with a dangerous instrument and:
        (i) He uses force against the person of anyone present with intent to overcome that person's physical resistance or physical power of resistance; or
        (ii) He threatens the imminent use of force against the person of anyone who is present with intent to compel acquiescence to the taking of or escaping with property.

[The statute then defines key terms and specifies the penalty for its violation]

The Japanese take a more common-sense approach to the question of what constitutes a crime, and while appellate courts do on occasion have to interpret a particular term, not a lot of time is spent on proving specific elements of the offense. Given the fact that there are no juries in Japan nor is there plea bargaining, and that most defendants confess, finely detailed penal statutes are not necessary. The question of degree of offense is dealt with in the sentence, not in the definition of the offense itself.

Although the Japanese Penal Code is in many respects quite similar to those found in many jurisdictions in the United States, it has some unique features as well. Punishments range from death by hanging through life imprisonment to minor fines, with sentences generally being indeterminate. Indeterminate sentences can range from one month to fifteen years, although aggravation can increase the term to twenty years and mitigation can reduce it to less than one month (Book I, Chapter II). Sentences may be suspended, with the convicted person either being free or on probation (Chapter IV, Article 25), and once incarcerated the convict is eligible for parole after having served one-third of his sentence, or ten years in the case of a life sentence (Chapter V, Article 28). Should the punishment specified in the sentence not be executed within a statutorily limited period of time, the person is exempted from that punishment. The statutory limits for imprisonment range from thirty years for a death penalty to one year for penal detention, minor fine, or confiscation (Chapter VI). The Penal Code contains the standard provisions regarding justifiable acts and defenses of insanity, infancy (fourteen years or younger), etc., but Article 42 of Chapter VII also provides for leniency for those who surrender before being identified as the responsible party.

Inasmuch as the Penal Code is a national law, it includes offenses ranging from insurrection to obstructing traffic. Interestingly enough, however, while the code punishes insurrection and aiding foreign aggression (Chapters II and III of Book II, respectively), it does not provide for the offense of espionage as such. This is especially ironic given the fact the code (Book II, Chapter XIII) punishes those who disclose professional secrets (doctors, lawyers, pharmacists, etc.). The issue is being debated in the Diet, and it is not unlikely that such a law will be passed in the near future, especially given the increasing exchange of military technology with the United States. The usual crimes involving bodily injury are found (Chapter XXVII), but a specific chapter (XXVIII) covers bodily injury and death through negligence, including death or bodily injury through negligence in the conduct of one's occupation, with sentences ranging up to five years at forced labor. Construction foremen and even owners of companies or managers of hotels have been sentenced under this article for injury or death caused by their negligence. Abortion in Japan is technically illegal, punishable by up to seven years at forced labor (Chapter XXIX), but the Eugenic Protection Law (*Yūsei Hogo Hō*) allows qualified physicians to perform abortions in several types of cases, the most common of which is where the continuation of the pregnancy or labor would cause extreme deterioration of the mother's health for physical or economic reasons. It is usually the economic factor that is used as a justification for the abortion.

Japan is well known as a nation that prohibits private ownership of handguns. The law controlling possession of firearms and swords covers such offenses, providing punishments of up to ten years at forced labor for violations. Although hunting rifles and shotguns are not prohibited, possession and use is strictly controlled (see Ames 1981: 140-41). The same holds true for swords, still an integral part of Japanese culture. The primary offenders of these statutes are members of organized crime, as will be discussed below. Separate laws covering drugs are quite similar to those found in the United States and other countries, as are laws governing the operation of motor vehicles.

CRIME IN JAPAN

Crime rates in Japan are very low. This fact very likely accounts for the scholarly studies of Japanese police and for many not-so-scholarly articles in the popular press. Anyone who has spent any time in Japan cannot but be struck by the lack of apparent crime and by the general feeling of safety that this engenders. Shop owners routinely leave merchandise on stands outside their shops unattended, thousands of bicycles are left daily at train and sub-way stations unsecured or locked only by a flimsy handlebar lock, and stores rarely have anti-shoplifting detection devices, although the larger department stores have store detectives. Unescorted women can use buses or subways at any time without fear, although they may have to fend off inebriated businessmen on their way home from the normal drinking bout after work. People can walk the streets at any time of day or night with little fear of crime. This feeling of security particularly affects foreigners. In a 1987 study by the Council for Public Policy in Japan it was found that almost 72 percent of those foreigners surveyed felt no great anxiety about crime, and only 14 percent had been victims of any crime (*White Paper on Police 1987:* 10-11). The most frequent crimes reported by foreigners were thefts and lascivious and other sexual crimes.[3] I can attest to this feeling of safety and general amazement at the great opportunity for, but general lack of, crime. There is, then, a feeling of security that is rarely found in Western industrialized countries, a feeling that is supported by statistics.

Figure 1.1 compares reported major offenses among five nations: Japan, Federal Republic of Germany, France, United Kingdom, and the United States. Inasmuch as these figures are total numbers of crimes reported and not rates, they are population sensitive, and it would be expected that the United States, with the highest population, would have the most crimes. The population of Japan, however, is somewhat less than one-half that of the United States but clearly has far fewer than one-half the crimes. This disparity becomes more pronounced when we observe the rates of crime in these countries (see figure 1.2). The overall crime rate is higher in the three European countries than in the United States, but the crime rate in the United States is almost four times the rate in Japan. When this is broken down into individual offenses, as in table 1.1, we can see that the United States has the highest rate of violent offenses and that Japan is quite low in all categories, although its murder rate is closer to the rates of the other countries than its rate for other offenses. A significant percentage of these murders involve infanticide,[4] a phenomenon not found in the other countries to the extent it is found in Japan (Kumasaka et al. 1975:23-24). Just as striking as the low crime rates are the clearance rates, or crimes solved by arrest, for the five nations. Japan has clearance rates (table 1.1) much higher than the other countries. There are, of course, numerous problems associated with crime statistics. Many crimes are underreported, definitions of crimes vary from jurisdiction to jurisdiction, and reporting methods often differ as well. It is especially difficult to accurately compare crime statistics cross-nationally (Kumasaka et al. 1975: 19-20). Victimization studies have become quite common in the United States, giving researchers as well as the public a more comprehensive picture of the true crime rate. Crime, it turns

Figure 1.1
Trends in the Number of Reported Major Offenses (1976-1985)

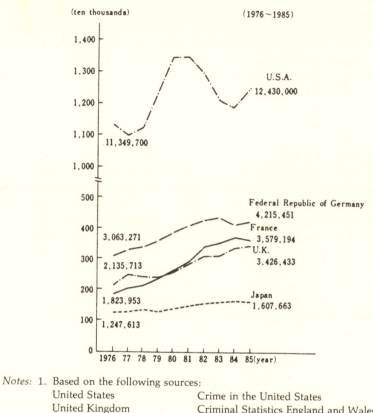

Notes: 1. Based on the following sources:

United States	Crime in the United States
United Kingdom	Criminal Statistics England and Wales
Federal Republic of Germany	Polizeiliche Kriminalstatistik
France	La criminalité en France
Japan	Statistics of the National Police Agency

    2. The number of reported offenses in the respective countries are based on the following criteria:

United States	Only Crime Index offenses (murder, aggravated assault, forcible rape, robbery, burglary, larceny—theft, and motor vehicle theft; in 1979, arson was added to Index offenses) are counted, and the figures are estimates.
United Kingdom	Only indicatable offenses until 1978 and notifiable offenses since 1979 are counted; based on statistics from England and Wales.
Federal Republic of Germany	The number of *Straftat* is counted, excluding traffic offences and *Staatsschutz-delikte*.
France	The number of *crime et délit* is counted, excluding traffic offenses.
Japan	Penal code offenses other than traffic professional negligence.

Source: Government of Japan, Ministry of Justice, Research and Training Institute, "Summary of White Paper on Crime" (1987), p. 7.

Figure 1.2
Crime Rate and Clearance Rate of Major Offenses (1985)

①Crime Rate   ②Clearance Rate

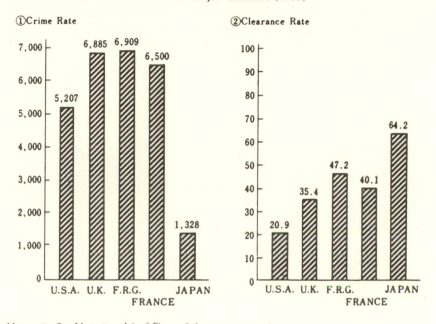

Notes: 1. See Note 1 and 2 of Figure 1.1.
       2. "Crime Rate" means the number of reported offenses per 100,000 population.

Source: Government of Japan, Ministry of Justice, Research and Training Institute, "Summary of White Paper on Crime" (1987), p. 8.

out, is generally underreported, with some offenses much more so than others. Victimization surveys are not as common in Japan, however, so we are not as sure to what extent crime is underreported there, but studies that have been done in Japan indicate that the underreporting problem is not as great in Japan as it is in the United States (Bayley 1976: 6-8; Parker 1984: 16-17, 100). Thus, the disparity in crime rates between the two countries is probably even greater than the figures cited indicate. It is my opinion after having lived in Japan that the differences are greater than the statistics would indicate.

Despite the low crime rate in Japan, crime is still perceived as a major problem and it worries the citzens. There is particular concern about organized crime, juvenile delinquency, and crimes by radical groups. Organized crime by "bōryokudan" (organized crime) gangs takes the form of gambling, extortion, smuggling, and drugs, and while a good deal of bōryokudan violence is directed at rival gangs, the criminal activities of these groups nevertheless have a significant impact on the average citizen.

Table 1.1
International Comparison of Number of Crimes Known to Police, Crime Rate, and Clearance Rate (1987)

Category	Japan	U.S.A.	Britain	West Germany	France
Population	121,672,000	241,077,000	49,923,500	61,047,700	55,279,100
Homicide					
Number of cases	1,676	20,613	2,160	2,728	2,413
Crime rate	1.4	8.6	4.3	4.5	4.4
Clearance rate (%)	96.7	70.2	76.7	93.9	89.4
Robbery					
Number of cases	1,949	542,775	30,020	28,581	50,740
Crime rate	1.6	225.1	60.1	46.8	91.8
Clearance rate (%)	78.5	24.7	20.4	48.4	24.0
Rape					
Number of cases	1,750	90,434	5,205	5,604	2,937
Crime rate	1.4	37.5	10.4	9.2	5.3
Clearance rate (%)	88.1	52.3	78.3	70.8	81.6
Larceny					
Number of cases	1,375,096	11,722,700	2,893,996	2,720,077	2,041,268
Crime rate	1,130.2	4,862.6	5,796.9	4,455.7	3,692.7
Clearance rate (%)	58.7	17.5	28.3	28.9	15.3
Larceny on premises					
Number of cases	296,777	3,241,410	931,620	1,647,658	409,858
Crime rate	243.9	1,344.6	1,866.1	2,699.0	741.4
Clearance ratge (%)	70.8	13.6	26.0	17.2	14.3

Notes: 1. Source: Statistics of criminal offenses compiled in respective countries.
        2. Here, Britain comprises England and Wales.
        3. The figures representing the larceny in the statistics of West Germany are those of aggravated larceny.

Source: Government of Japan, National Police Agency, "White Paper on Police 1988" (excerpt), p. 130.

As of the end of 1987, there were 3,201 organized gangs with a combined membership of 86,287. About 37 percent of the groups were affiliated with the three main gangs: *Yamaguchi-gumi, Inagawa-kai,* and *Sumiyoshi-rengōkai* (*White Paper on Police 1987:* 47). In 1987, 88 percent of the 164 known incidents of inter-gang violence involved firearms, resulting in 18 deaths and 35 injuries (*White Paper on Police 1988:* 28). Firearms are strictly regulated in Japan, and the possession of handguns is absolutely forbidden, so the smuggling of these weapons is a major *bōryokudan* industry. A total of 1,299 handguns were seized from *bōryokudan* members in 1986. The total number of deaths attributed to firearms in Japan in 1987 was 39,[5] with organized crime accounting for approximately 46 percent of those deaths (ibid.). Also in 1987, 30 percent of the 493 homicides cleared in Japan were committed by *bōryokudan* members (*White Paper on Crime 1988:* 70). Offenses by *bōryokudan* were concentrated among a relatively small number of specific crimes: they accounted for 65 percent of the intimidation cases, 41 percent of the extortion cases, 35 percent of gambling cases, and 30 percent of the homicide cases, and with respect to special law crimes, they accounted for 65 percent of the Bicycle Race Law offenses, 53 percent of the Horse Race Law offenses, and 45 percent of the Stimulant Drug Control Law offenses (ibid.: 10). Organized crime, or *bōryokudan*, offenses are showing a downward trend despite the increasing publicity about their activities. From a peak of 82,704 offenses cleared in 1956 to a low of 38,180 in 1969 and another peak of 58,750 in 1978, the trend has been downward, with 40,257 reported in 1987 (ibid.: 69).[6]

Although the likelihood of being victimized by crime in Japan is quite low, citizen awareness of crime is relatively high. Serious offenses are widely reported, both in the newspapers and on television, and reports of offenses that would appear only in local or metropolitan newspapers in the United States appear in national newspapers in Japan. Armed robberies, for example, are so rare that they are virtually always reported in the media across Japan regardless of the site of the crime; kidnappings and murders receive even more attention, as one might expect.[7] There are several "cops and robbers" television programs, and soap operas often involve crime. A series of kidnap-murders in 1988 and 1989 attracted a great deal of publicity, because they involved young girls (seven to ten years) as victims and an offender who wrote letters (and in one case sent the remains of a victim) to the parents of the victims. The publicity continued after the arrest of a suspect (who, it should be added, confessed almost immediately), and there was considerable discussion about the need for parents to keep a much closer watch on their children. Details about the suspect and his crimes that would have jeopardized an American defendant's right to a fair trial were given in the newspapers. There is no jury system in Japan, thus allowing much greater media freedom in reporting crime. Such freedom in reporting may increase the awareness of crime, suggesting that there is more crime than statistics would indicate. Because serial killers are extremely rare in Japan and this case was in many ways unprecedented, there was exceptional publicity.

Table 1.2 illustrates the number of penal code offenses reported to and cleared by police in 1987, the latest year for which figures are available. Table 1.3 includes "Special Law Offenses," such as firearms and swords, stimulant drugs, or road-traffic violations, all of which are considered crimes but not included in the Penal Code. Many of the offenses listed are those commonly found in any penal code, but some are rather unique to Japan, such as "breach of trust" and "obstruction of performance of an official duty." Note the high clearance rates, which vary from over 100 percent (more crimes cleared than reported) to a low of 32.6 percent for "destruction of property" (vandalism). All of the serious offenses have very high

Table 1.2

Number of Penal Code Offenses Reported to and Cleared by the Police and
the Number of Offenders Cleared (1987)

Offence	Number of offences reported	Number of offences cleared	Number of offenders cleared	Clearance rate	Difference from the previous year	
					Number of offences reported	Number of offenders cleared
Total	2,132,592	1,566,713	983,891	73.5	8,353(0.4)	15,919(1.6)
Homicide	1,584	1,552	1,651	98.0	△ 92(5.5)	△ 41(2.4)
Robbery	1,874	1,465	1,707	78.2	△ 75(3.8)	△ 135(7.3)
Bodily injury	21,046	19,585	27,463	93.1	△ 125(0.6)	△ 917(3.2)
Assault	9,970	9,292	12,146	93.2	△ 838(7.8)	△ 1,616(11.7)
Intimidation	1,106	1,065	1,108	96.3	49(4.6)	169(18.0)
Extortion	11,855	9,951	11,196	83.9	△ 1,049(8.1)	△ 1,105(9.0)
Unlawful assembly with weapons	102	103	842	101.0	10(10.9)	14(1.7)
Larceny	1,364,796	821,831	261,934	60.2	△10,300(0.7)	1,401(0.5)
Fraud	69,844	67,784	13,566	97.1	5,056(7.8)	187(1.4)
Embezzlement	42,580	42,451	43,594	99.7	5,144(13.7)	6,105(16.3)
Breach of trust	87	87	105	100.0	△ 6(6.5)	△ 12(10.3)
Purchase, etc. of stolen property	2,074	2,072	1,916	99.9	△ 28(1.3)	115(6.4)
Rape	1,823	1,593	1,608	87.4	73(4.2)	31(2.0)
Indecent assault	2,404	1,824	1,046	75.9	113(4.9)	△ 59(5.3)
Public indecency	983	957	910	97.4	△ 90(8.4)	△ 41(4.3)
Distribution of obscene literature, etc.	1,202	1,202	1,105	100.0	△ 161(11.8)	23(2.1)
Arson	1,814	1,589	836	87.6	38(2.1)	△ 60(6.7)
Fire caused by negligence	933	717	687	76.8	△ 169(15.3)	△ 164(19.3)
Bribery	328	329	487	100.3	△ 14(4.1)	51(11.7)
Kidnapping	106	103	84	97.2	△ 7(6.2)	△ 1(1.2)
Obstruction of the performance of an official duty	1,209	1,209	1,048	100.0	△ 92(7.1)	△ 72(6.4)
House-breaking	11,776	5,149	3,310	43.7	△ 788(6.3)	114(3.6)
Destruction of property	11,976	3,903	2,758	32.6	937(8.5)	△ 44(1.6)
Forgery and counterfeiting	11,899	11,813	1,574	99.3	△ 1,187(9.1)	△ 149(8.6)
Gambling	2,122	2,127	8,990	100.2	383(22.0)	1,309(17.0)
Violent acts	75	70	148	93.3	19(33.9)	36(32.1)
Traffic professional negligence	554,663	554,663	579,169	100.0	11,802(2.2)	11,058(1.9)
Others	2,361	2,227	2,903	94.3	△ 250(9.6)	△ 278(8.7)

Notes: 1. Clearance rate = $\dfrac{\text{number of offenses cleared}}{\text{number of offenses reported}} \times 100$

Some clearance rates may exceed 100.0% as offenses reported prior to, but cleared during, 1986 are counted.

2. Figures in parentheses show the percentage of increase or decrease.

3. △ indicates a decrease.

Source: National Police Agency from Government of Japan, Ministry of Justice, Research and Training Institute, "Summary of White Paper on Crime" (1987), p. 5.

14

Table 1.3
Number of Special Law Offenders Received by the Public Prosecutor's
Office (1986, 1987)

Offence		1986	1987	Difference from the previous year	
				Number	Rate of increase or decrease
Total		2,323,042	1,635,506	Δ687,536	Δ 29.6
Election Law		14,995	21,113	6,118	40.8
Traffic	Road Transport Law	654	892	238	36.4
	Vehicles Law	2,594	2,636	42	1.6
	Automobile Compensation Law	2,888	2,539	Δ 349	Δ 12.1
	Road Traffic Law	2,102,078	1,455,059	Δ647,019	Δ 30.8
	Law Concerning Places to Keep Automobiles, etc.	83,527	45,221	Δ 38,306	Δ 45.9
Preservation of public peace	Fire arms and swords	5,081	4,837	Δ 244	Δ 4.8
	Gunpowder Control Law	502	462	Δ 40	Δ 8.0
	Minor Offences Law	6,055	4,484	Δ 1,571	Δ 25.9
	Nuisance by drunken persons	679	608	Δ 71	Δ 10.5
Finance and economy	Income Tax Law	107	81	Δ 26	Δ 24.3
	Corporation Tax Law	262	222	Δ 40	Δ 15.3
	Customs Law	306	435	129	42.2
	Investment Law	447	341	Δ 106	Δ 23.7
	Land and Building Trade Law	292	237	Δ 55	Δ 18.8
	Unfair Competition Prevention Law	61	55	Δ 6	Δ 9.8
Drugs	Narcotics	194	154	Δ 40	Δ 20.6
	Opium	169	156	Δ 13	Δ 7.7
	Cannabis	1,516	1,511	Δ 5	Δ 0.3
	Stimulant drugs	28,699	27,214	Δ 1,485	Δ 5.2
	Poisonous substances	24,051	23,423	Δ 628	Δ 2.6
Public morals	Anti-Prostitution Law	3,464	3,180	Δ 284	Δ 8.2
	Public morals	5,128	4,471	Δ 657	Δ 12.8
	Employment Security Law	225	289	64	28.4
	Child Welfare Law	953	880	Δ 73	Δ 7.7
	Horse Race Law	2,036	1,672	Δ 364	Δ 17.9
	Bicycle Race Law	770	373	Δ 397	Δ 51.6
Foreigners	Alien Registration Law	3,120	2,438	Δ 682	Δ 21.9
	Immigration control	808	938	130	16.1
Local autonomy ordinances	Public Security Ordinance	28	19	Δ 9	Δ 32.1
	Others	5,389	4,930	Δ 459	Δ 8.5
Others		25,964	24,636	Δ 1,328	Δ 5.1

Notes: 1. Figures for Election Law include offenses related to elections or voting stipulated by the Fishery Law and the Local Autonomy Law.
    2. Δ indicates a decrease.

Source: Annual Statistics Report of Prosecution from Government of Japan, Ministry of Justice, Research and Training Institute, "Summary of the White Paper on Crime" (1988), p. 7.

clearance rates compared to the United States. Note also the two-year trend is a decrease in crime, the only significant exceptions being in sex offenses, arson, gambling, and white collar crimes. The same basic trends hold true when we examine the "special law offenses," involving firearms, swords, and drugs, for example.

Although the adult crime rate is stable or even declining somewhat, juvenile crime in Japan is becoming a major problem and is perceived as rising significantly. In the first half of 1989, more crimes were committed by minors (ages fourteen through nineteen) than by adults, a first ever in Japan (*The Japan Times* 8/13/89: 18). Table 1.4 illustrates the trend of juvenile offenses cleared, with the rate per 1,000 population rising from 10.7 in 1978 to 14.3 in 1981 and 1982, and then declining through 1987. The number of juvenile offenses, as opposed to those cleared, however, is rising. The vast majority of crimes committed by juveniles are larcenies (75.9 percent in 1987), with crimes of violence being relatively rare. There is very likely substantial underreporting of juvenile violence, however. Much of it takes place in or around the school, and while it may be passed off as "bullying,"[8] the violence is nevertheless quite real. Victims are reluctant to report such incidents for fear of retaliation and school authorities prefer to handle known incidents internally rather than damaging the reputation of the school through the use of police in cases that do not involve serious bodily injury. There were 403 juveniles contacted by the police in Japan in 1987 for "guidance" on bullying, down from 845 the previous year (*White Paper on Police 1988:* 57). There were 482 cases of violence against teachers reported in 1987, down from 627 in 1986; neither are large numbers in overall terms, but such violence constitutes a problem that worries parents and teachers alike. This offense may be declining, however, because the number of cases has gone down each year since 1984 (*White Paper on Police 1987:* 57). On the other hand, while assaults against teachers seems to be declining, assaults by teachers on students seems to be increasing. There are laws prohibiting corporal punishment, but they are rarely enforced unless severe injury or death occurs, and the striking of students by teachers and coaches in Japan is commonly accepted (*The Sunday Star-Bulletin and Advertiser* 5/21/89: E-3). Filial violence is also an increasing problem in Japan, most often taking the form of fifteen- or sixteen-year-old males committing violent acts against their mothers. Although there have been few systematic studies of such violence, the evidence that exists points to a serious but previously hidden problem. Such violent acts tend to be committed by youths from families with high socioeconomic status who attend prestigious public or private schools (Kumagai 1983: 178-83). This may be a function of the extreme pressure to succeed by entering a top university that such children are under.

Drug abuse in the form of inhaling volatile fluids (classified as "thinner" by authorities but including many different organic solvents, all capable of

Table 1.4

Number of Juvenile Penal Code Offenders Excluding Traffic Professional Negligence Cleared by the Police and Rate per Population, by Age Group (1978-1987)

Year	Total			Under 14 years old (child offender)		14~15 years old		16~17 years old		18~19 years old	
	Number	Rate per popu-lation	Per-cent-age of juve-niles	Number	Rate per popu-lation	Number	Rate per popu-lation	Number	Rate per popu-lation	Number	Rate per popu-lation
1978	177,719	10.7	42.0	40,918	5.9	60,325	18.2	51,078	16.1	25,398	7.9
1979	184,839	10.9	45.1	41,681	5.9	66,258	19.1	51,744	16.0	25,156	8.0
1980	219,956	12.8	49.3	53,883	7.2	80,241	24.8	58,158	17.5	27,674	8.8
1981	252,808	14.3	52.0	67,906	8.9	94,169	28.5	64,530	18.6	26,203	8.1
1982	257,856	14.3	50.8	65,926	8.4	103,756	28.0	61,329	18.9	26,845	8.1
1983	261,634	14.1	52.0	64,851	8.1	110,433	29.5	59,468	18.0	26,882	7.7
1984	248,540	13.2	49.5	55,875	6.9	103,451	27.1	62,931	17.0	26,283	8.1
1985	250,132	13.1	51.2	56,015	6.9	103,729	26.5	65,532	17.5	24,856	7.5
1986	235,176	12.1	52.3	49,803	6.3	97,126	24.2	63,168	16.5	25,079	6.8
1987	227,978	11.8	51.2	40,786	5.4	92,788	22.6	66,616	17.1	27,788	7.4

Notes: 1. Penal Code offenses include violations of the Law Punishing Use of Glass Bottle Grenades, and the Law Punishing Activities Endangering Civil Aviation.

2. Rate per population for child offenders means the number of child Penal Code offenders cleared per 1,000 children aged 10 through 13; and rate per population for juvenile offenders means the number of juvenile Penal Code offenders cleared per 1,000 juveniles in each age group.

Sources: National Policy Agency and Statistics Bureau, Management and Coordination Agency from Government of Japan, Ministry of Justice, Research and Training Institute, "Summary of the White Paper on Crime" (1988), p. 132.

producing an intoxicating effect) is not only increasing as a crime but is resulting in an increasing number of deaths as well. There were 22,381 juveniles referred to the prosecutor by the police in 1987 for this offense. Use of stimulant drugs (generally methamphetamine) is not widespread among the juvenile population; 1,502 students were contacted by the police about such use in 1987 (*White Paper on Crime 1988:* 135). The trend in stimulant drug offenses among the general population in Japan, however, has been on the rise since the late 1960s, where it had remained steady for over ten years after hitting a high of 53,221 in 1954 and then dropping drastically the following year to 271 (ibid.: 75). Despite the upward trend of such offenses in recent years, the number of drug offenses cleared in 1985 was still amost one-half the number cleared in 1954. "Hot-rodders," or *bōsōzoku*, on motorcycles, are responsible for increasing numbers of nses, ranging from murder to traffic law violations, but most crimes among these groups are nonviolent (Parker 1984: 144-45). The *bōsōzuku* generally cruise around at night and on the weekends, creating a great deal of noise and annoyance. The mortality rate among these groups is high, because they take great delight in racing each other and taunting police and trying to outrun them, a task that is not too difficult given the mismatch between the very fast motorcycles and the rather slow sedans used by Japanese police. Unfortunately, all too often these contests end in death or serious injury for the motorcyclist. The large majority of *bōsōzoku* are young "salarymen" or high school students (Ames 1981: 84-85), and many of these motorcycle enthusiasts are attracted to police work due to the opportunity to be on the motorcycle squad (ibid.: 155).

To keep these problems in perspective, it should be noted that while juvenile delinquency is increasing in Japan and is seen as a serious problem, it is insignificant when compared to juvenile delinquency in the United States, both in terms of amount and in terms of seriousness. Most juvenile delinquency in Japan occurs among junior high school students, with the rates declining as the student passes into high school and beyond, unlike patterns in the United States, and authorities are making concerted efforts to reverse the trend of increasing crime among juveniles.

Although Japan's radical groups have not been particularly active in recent years, they are a concern for law enforcement authorities. As figure 1.3 indicates, there may be an upward trend in the number of incidents per year. There is a great potential for violence, however, and substantial measures are taken by Japanese authorities to keep track of and to control these radical groups. Infiltration, however, does not seem to be an acceptable method of intelligence-gathering by Japanese authorities. Ultra-leftist groups have memberships totaling about 35,000 and are becoming more sophisticated in the fabrication and use of explosive devices, although few citizens have been killed by them. The increasing activity by ultra-leftists has been met by a response from the right, and clashes between the two are becoming more common, although most clashes involve leftists rather than ultra-leftists. There are increasing numbers of factional conflicts among the ultra-leftists as well, some resulting in serious injury and death (*White Paper on Police 1988*: 11-12). Several members of the infamous Japanese Red Army[9] were recently arrested in Japan, an indication that the Middle Eastern group may be targeting Japan for violence or using Japan as a base for attacking other targets in Asia. Right-wing groups do not seem to constitute as much of a threat as do the leftists, and although they are highly visible are not paid much attention by the police. The rightists have been particularly active in harassing the Japan Teachers' Union (*Nikkyōso*) with everything from sound trucks (a favorite rightist tool) to short swords and smoke bombs.

It is difficult to discern any geographical patterns with respect to crime in Japan. Table 1.5 gives crime rates for five offenses by prefecture. While

Figure 1.3
Trend of "Guerrilla" Incidents (1978-1987)

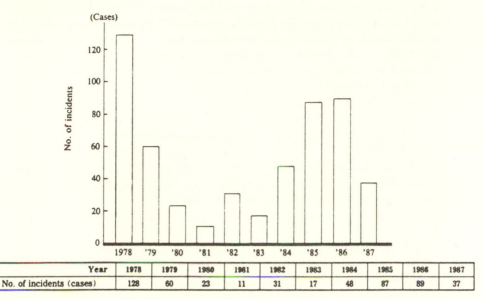

Year	1978	1979	1980	1981	1982	1983	1984	1985	1986	1987
No. of incidents (cases)	128	60	23	11	31	17	48	87	89	37

Source: Government of Japan, National Police Agency, "White Paper on Police 1988" (excerpt), p. 10.

Tokyo seems to have high rates for the offenses of robbery, bodily injury (assault), and larceny, it does not rank at the top in murder or stimulant drug offenses. Density of population does not seem to necessarily correlate with crime rate; Hokkaido, with quite low population density, has high rates of bodily injury, larceny, and stimulant drug offenses. Japan as a whole, of course, has a high population density, over 300 persons per square kilometer in 1981, with the density in some areas of Tokyo reaching over 20,000 persons per square kilometer. Using another measure, population per square kilometer of arable land, the comparative figures in 1980 were: Japan, 2,256; Indonesia, 1,019; West Germany, 820; United States, 103; and Australia, 30 (Young 1983: 67). It would seem, then, that one factor frequently mentioned as being related to, if not causative of, crime—population density—does not seem to be related to crime rate in Japan.[10] Some have suggested that population density in Japan has forced the Japanese to live together in harmony, as the alternative would be chaos and anarchy.

Long-term crime trends in Japan as depicted graphically show a remarkably flat line (see figure 1.1). While there has been a gradual upward trend since the mid-1970s, the trend until 1988 had been downward.[11] Clearance rates have remained even steadier over the years, and are quite high, as noted above. It is interesting to note the trends in the countries included;

Table 1.5
Prefectures and Crime—Rankings

Prefecture (by pop.)	Murder	Robbery	Larceny	Drugs	Bod. Inj.
1 Tokyo	18	2	1	11	2
2 Osaka	7	6	2	16	8
3 Kanagawa	12	3	11	21	6
4 Aichi	36	19	17	40	45
5 Saitama	34	9	20	34	41
6 Hokkaido	24	8	3	4	5
7 Hyogo	13	11	14	25	20
8 Chiba	25	7	12	26	37
9 Fukuoka	3	4	6	17	4
10 Shizuoka	27	10	25	15	46
11 Hiroshima	17	23	8	18	21
12 Ibaraki	23	20	23	14	13
13 Kyoto	37	5	13	10	7
14 Niigata	29	13	28	39	36
15 Miyagi	39	17	27	36	43
16 Nagano	43	40	29	33	33
17 Fukushima	42	26	21	24	25
18 Gifu	45	30	44	42	47
19 Gumma	20	25	22	3	39
20 Okayama	9	14	15	6	24
21 Tochigi	44	28	24	12	27
22 Kumamoto	6	33	43	20	14
23 Kagoshima	26	31	36	43	12
24 Mie	30	34	42	31	34
25 Yamaguchi	5	15	26	13	22
26 Nagasaki	15	39	46	32	3
27 Ehime	8	36	7	5	15
28 Aomori	31	22	33	28	16
29 Iwate	40	32	47	46	29
30 Nara	21	43	16	22	35
31 Yamagata	47	47	41	41	30
32 Oita	14	27	34	30	11
33 Akita	35	45	31	44	31
34 Okinawa	2	1	4	47	1
35 Shiga	32	37	19	23	40
36 Miyazaki	22	44	37	35	38
37 Ishikawa	41	35	35	27	28
38 Toyama	46	46	39	38	42
39 Wakayama	4	29	18	1	23
40 Kagawa	10	12	5	2	19
41 Saga	19	38	32	7	26
42 Yamanishi	33	18	40	19	17
43 Kochi	1	24	9	9	9
44 Tokushima	11	16	10	8	17
45 Fukui	38	41	45	37	44
46 Shimane	28	42	38	45	32
47 Tottori	16	21	30	29	10

Source: Government of Japan, Ministry of Justice, Research and Training Institute, "Summary of the White Paper on Crime" (1986), p. 16.

Japan has the flattest line, while the United Kingdom, France, and the Federal Republic of Germany have relatively steady and gradual upward trends and the United States has a rather skewed curve reflecting substantial increases as well as decreases in reported offenses, with the trend since 1984 being upward. Later we will explore the possible explanations of the low crime rate in Japan, but it is safe to state now that there is in fact a much lower crime rate in Japan than in comparable industrialized nations, East or West, and that the trend is not clearly upward, as in most other countries.[12] This low crime rate has a significant impact on Japan's criminal justice system; whether the criminal justice system has a significant impact on the crime rate, however, remains to be seen.

2

Law Enforcement

A fair amount has been written about Japanese police, reflecting the recent interest in all facets of Japanese society.[13] The reader is encouraged to read these studies as a means of learning about Japan today, but there is really no substitute for actually experiencing Japan firsthand as a resident, something not many of us have had the opportunity to do. The same holds true with respect to the police: it is difficult to understand Japanese police officers (or any police, for that matter) without actually either being one or working in close proximity to them for extended periods of time. Japanese police pose a special problem for Westerners, of course, with most of that problem revolving around language. Some of those who have studied Japanese police have been fluent in Japanese, but most have not, and so it is difficult to determine just how valid the various studies of Japanese police tend to be. Rather than attempt to determine this, we shall instead find areas of consensus among the various researchers and assume that this consensus is indicative of a certain degree of validity, as well as rely on the author's own research and impressions.

Japanese police are governed by The Police Law (*Keisatsu Hō*). This law not only establishes the duty and authority of the police, it establishes the structure of law enforcement throughout Japan. Thus, law enforcement in Japan is centralized, and there is no separate federal agency, such as the FBI in the United States. There is, however, prefectural autonomy in operations and recruitment, although all prospective police officers must meet basic standards established at the national level (Aichi Prefectural Police 1986: 7). The overall picture, then, is one of local control with a high degree of centralization in matters of policy, personnel, and equipment. Perhaps the best way to understand the relationship between the central authority and the prefectures is by examining figures 2.1, 2.2., and 2.3.

As may be seen in figure 2.1, the highest direct authority over the police is the National Public Safety Commission (*Kokka Kōan Iinkai*), which is in charge of "police operations relating to the public safety of the nation, administer[ing] affairs concerning police education, police communication, criminal identification, criminal statistics, and police equipment, as well as coordinat[ing] affairs concerning police administration." (The Police Law, Article 5, Section 1). The commission consists of six members, appointed by the prime minister and approved by both houses of the Diet; the chairman is a minister of state (without portfolio) (ibid., Articles 6 and 7). Their term of office is five years, with reappointment possible, and the members must not have been professional public servants in either police or prosecution for five years preceding their appointment, nor may more than two be members of the same political party (ibid., Article 7). It would seem, then, that the police are relatively independent of political influence from a structural point of view. This, in fact, seems to be the case in practice as well, although it is difficult to determine to what extent the conservative policies of the police are inherent in the job itself and to what extent they reflect the policies of the conservative ruling party (the Liberal Democratic Party, which is not so aptly named). Members of the National Public Safety Commission as well as of the prefectural commissions tend to be old and conservative, regardless of political affiliation (Ames 1981: 219).

The National Police Agency, or NPA (*Keisatsuchō*), located in Tokyo, is concerned with planning, research, coordination, and supervision. Figure 2.1 implies that the NPA has operational functions, as it contains criminal investigation divisions and a criminal investigation bureau, and takes charge of matters concerning international criminal investigation assistance and the prevention of crimes, but in reality it serves a staff function and offers coordination and supervision in a general sense only, not becoming involved in specific cases (The Police Law, Article 23; J. Crim. Pol.: 6-8). There are also attached organizations that carry out specific functions associated with law enforcement, including security for the emperor and his family. The head of the NPA is the commissioner general (*Keisatsuchō chōkan*), who is appointed by the National Public Safety Commission with the approval of the prime minister (Police Law, Article 16). In practice, however, the commissioner general is selected by his predecessor in consultation with the prime minister and selected members of his cabinet (Ames 1981: 220).

The NPA, in addition to assisting the prefectures in operational matters, establishes standards for the size and structure of prefectural police forces, recruitment and training of police officers, and general law enforcement

Figure 2.1
Organization of the National Police Agency

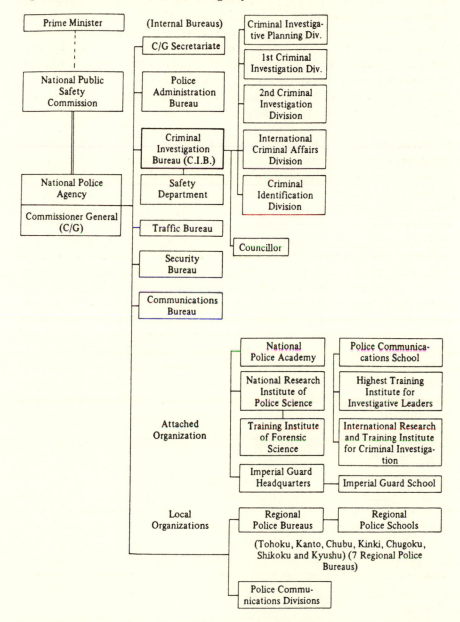

(Internal Bureaus)

Prime Minister

National Public Safety Commission

National Police Agency

Commissioner General (C/G)

C/G Secretariate

Police Administration Bureau

Criminal Investigation Bureau (C.I.B.)

Safety Department

Traffic Bureau

Security Bureau

Communications Bureau

Criminal Investigative Planning Div.

1st Criminal Investigation Div.

2nd Criminal Investigation Division

International Criminal Affairs Division

Criminal Identification Division

Councillor

Attached Organization

National Police Academy

National Research Institute of Police Science

Training Institute of Forensic Science

Imperial Guard Headquarters

Police Communications School

Highest Training Institute for Investigative Leaders

International Research and Training Institute for Criminal Investigation

Imperial Guard School

Local Organizations

Regional Police Bureaus

Regional Police Schools

(Tohoku, Kanto, Chubu, Kinki, Chugoku, Shikoku and Kyushu) (7 Regional Police Bureaus)

Police Communications Divisions

Source: Government of Japan, National Police Agency, "Japanese Criminal Police" (1985), p. 9.

policy. Ranks are standard throughout Japan (see table 2.1). Regional police bureaus, of which there are seven, fall under the NPA and serve as local organs of the agency (see figure 2.2). They carry out most of the functions of the NPA on a regional basis and help to coordinate police matters and crimes that are inter-prefectural in nature, as well as operate regional police schools that train higher-ranking police officials. Each regional bureau has jurisdiction over four (Shikoku region) to ten (Kanto region) prefectures. Hokkaido (the northern-most island) is like a prefecture itself, and therefore does not have a regional police bureau, and Tokyo, due to its size and the special nature of the Tokyo Metropolitan Police, is excluded from the Kanto Regional Police Bureau (J. Crim. Pol.: 11).[14] In effect, both organizations play dual roles as regional and prefectural organizations.

The forty-seven prefectures, which are roughly equivalent to states in the United States or shires in the United Kingdom, each have a prefectural police force under a Prefectural Public Safety Commission. The commissions consist of three or five members, depending on the designation of the geographical area in question (Hokkaido, Tokyo, Osaka, and Kyoto have five; all the rest have three). Members of the commissions are appointed by the prefectural governor with the consent of the prefectural assembly, with essentially the same membership requirements as the national commission; their term of office is three years (Police Law, Articles 38-40). The chairman of each commission is elected by the members of the commission, and serves for one year. The prefectural commissions serve the same prupose with respect to the prefectural police departments as the national commission does with respect to the NPA, except that the prefectural commission

Table 2.1
Personnel by Rank: Aichi Prefecture

Superintendent Supervisor	(Keishikan)	1
Chief Superintendent	(Keishicho)	1
Senior Superintendent	(Keishisei)	24
Superintendent	(Keishi)	198
Police Inspector	(Keibu)	447
Assistant Police Inspector	(Keibuho)	1,573
Police Sergeant	(Junsabucho)	3,793
Senior Policeman	(Junsacho)	1,393
Policeman	(Junsa)	3,719
TOTAL		11,149

Source: Aichi Prefectural Police 1986, pp. 8-9.

Figure 2.2
Organization of the Kanto Regional Police Bureau

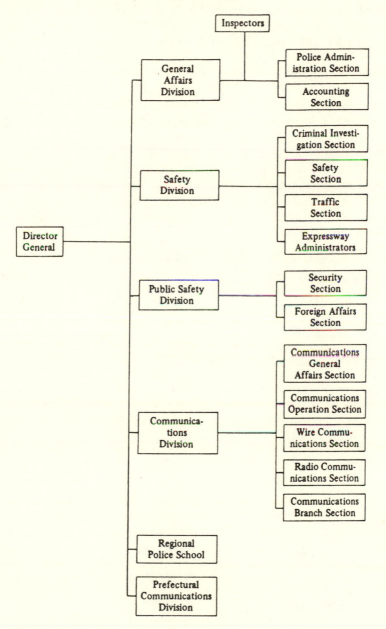

Source: Government of Japan, National Police Agency, "Japanese Criminal Police" (1985), p. 10.

does not appoint the head (chief) of the prefectural police deparment but rather "approves" the chief who is assigned by the NPA after formal appointment by the National Public Safety Commission (no prefectural commission has ever disapproved of a chief) (Ames 1981: 218). The chief of the prefectural police is an employee of the NPA and not of the prefecture, as are all police officials at the rank of senior superintendent (*Keishi Sei*) and above.[15] The NPA, and therefore the national treasury, funds not only the salaries of senior police officials in each prefecture but many other expenses as well, including police academies and other training facilities, communications equipment, criminal identification functions, vehicles, boats and aircraft, firearms, and the compilation of criminal statistics (Police Law, Article 37).

Unlike most other nations, Japan has a law setting forth the methods by which a police officer must carry out his duties, the Police Duties Execution Law (*Keisatsukan Shokummu Shikkō Hō*, effective 1948, as revised). This, in addition to the Code of Criminal Procedure previously cited, provides the statutory authority for a great deal of police activity. Article 2, for example, deals with questioning:

> A police officer may stop and question any person who has reasonable ground to be suspected of having committed or is about to commit a crime judging from his or her unusual behavior and/or other surrounding circumstances, or who is deemed to have some information on the crime which has already been committed or is about to be committed.
>
> In cases when a police officer considers that such questioning on the spot as that provided for in the preceding paragraph will disadvantage the subject person or obstruct traffic, he may ask him or her to come with him to a nearby police station, police box, or residential police box for questioning.
>
> Any person provided for in the preceding two paragraphs shall not be detained, or forced to be taken to a police station or police box or a residential police box or compelled to answer his questions against his or her will so long as it is not based on the laws concerning criminal procedure.
>
> With regard to the person who is under arrest in accordance with laws concerning criminal procedure, a police officer may search his or her person for any possible weapon.

The law formalizes probable cause, and questions as to proper police procedure are answered primarily by reference to this law as well as the Constitution rather than upon appellate court decisions. Other provisions of the law deal with taking suspects into custody, emergency entry into buildings, vehicles, etc., and the use of weapons.

RECRUITMENT AND TRAINING

The police officer, of course, learns how to do his job not from such statutes but rather from formal training and experience. The formal training of a police officer starts soon after recruitment. Both recruitment policies and training determine the nature of the new police officer. Prospective police officers must pass a standardized "Examination for Police Officers," consisting of multiple-choice questions testing general knowledge and an essay question to test the applicant's reasoning and writing ability. Those who pass this test are then given a physical examiniation, an aptitude test, a psychological examination (Rorschach) and an interview. There is an extensive background check as well, and those from families with histories of mental illness, criminality, or left-wing affiliations will normally be disqualified (Ames 1981: 163-65; Charle 1979: 52). Applicants are divided into two groups—male high school graduates, and women and college or university graduates—with the former attending the prefectural police academy for twelve months and the latter for six months. Both receive essentially the same training, but it is more intense and less emphasis is placed on general education for the college graduates and women. There are usually eight to ten applicants for every position (Charle 1979: 52; Ames 1981: 165). There is also a program designed both to supply more mid-level administrators outside of normal promotion as well as to appeal to those who might not normally consider law enforcement as a career (Parker 2984: 133). Applicants for the position of assistant inspector (roughly equivalent to lieutenant in a police department in the United States) must have a college degree and pass an advanced civil service examination, in addition to meeting the requirements for the entry level position. Recruitment for this level position is conducted directly by the NPA and the one-year training course takes place at the National Police Academy (*Keisatsu Daigakkō*). Although such mid-level entry might appear to reduce the opportunities for promotion of sergeants and therefore adversely affect morale, the relatively small number of people recruited in this manner (usually about fifteen per year) has virtually no effect on promotion opportunities for sergeants, while at the same time providing a well-qualified group of mid-level officers who advance through the ranks much more rapidly than those who enter through the normal process (Ueno 1979: 12; Ames 1981: 184).[16]

The vast majority of police recruits attend a prefectural police school (or, in the case of Tokyo, the Metropolitan Police School). All recruits live in dormitories and have very little contact with the outside world. They attend classes and study approximately twelve hours per day (Hicks 1985: 73). There are four categories of study: general education (190 hours); law (158 hours); police activities (848 hours); and technical training (562 hours). Miscellaneous training takes 310 hours (hour figures for the one-year curriculum) (Ames 1981: 170-71).[17] The six-month course places less emphasis on general education and more on police training (ibid.). It is interesting to note that recruits spend 60 hours taking firearms training and 90 hours each on judo and kendo (Japanese fencing), and most obtain a black

belt in one of the traditional martial arts (Ames 1981. 170-71; Charle 1979:
52). Recruits also engage in club activities, much like the average college
student, where they practice tea ceremony, poetry, and calligraphy (Ames
1981: 171). Recruit training is rigorous, and despite the highly selective
nature of the initial recruitment, approximately 10 percent of the recruits
fail to complete the course (Ueno 1979: 15).

After graduation from the police school, the new officers are given three
months of on-the-job training at the police station to which they have been
assigned, and are then assigned to the field for another nine months, after
which they return to school for a four-month refresher course (Ueno 1979:
15). There is considerable in-service training for all officers to keep them
current on recent developments in the field, to give them specialized training in specific areas, and to prepare them for new assignments (ibid.: 15-16).
In-service training may take place in prefectural, regional, or national
police schools. Little emphasis is placed on firearms training after the initial
police school, but practice in judo and/or kendo is frequent and the annual
police competitions in these martial arts are major events (Ames 1981: 173;
Bayley 1976: 74). As the police officer progresses up the career ladder the
training continues unabated, but the emphasis shifts to administrative
skills. The emphasis on training not only results in a well-educated and
proficient police officer, but also breaks up the routine of police work that
can reduce morale and efficiency.

Female officers in Japan are generally assigned to the "traditionally
female" roles within departments, such as the juvenile and communications
divisions. They are not assigned to patrol and are not armed, although they
do perform traffic duty. By law, female officers cannot work after
10:30 P.M. They generally do not make a career of police work and, like the
rest of the female working population, are expected to get married by the
age of twenty-five or so.[18]

PROMOTION

Promotion through the rank of superintendent is based on examination
and time in grade. Time in grade (rank) requirements depend upon the entry
educational level of the officer; for sergeant, for example, the high school
graduate must spend four-and-one-half years in grade while the college
graduate must spend only two years. The differential decreases from
sergeant to assistant inspector (three and two years) and is eliminated
altogether after that, with four years required in grade to make inspector
and nine years for superintendent (Aichi Prefectural Police 1986: 8). The
examinations combine written tests and oral interviews. After the rank of
superintendent, promotion is by recommendation of senior officers (Bayley
1976: 60).

After passing the required examinations and being selected for promotion, the candidate is sent to the appropriate school (regional schools for sergeants and assistant inspectors, National Police Academy for higher ranks) for training. The course for sergeant lasts ten weeks, six of which are in a general course in leadership and four of which are in specialized training, with prospective sergeants selecting one of four curricula: criminal investigation, crime prevention, traffic control, and public security. The course for assistant inspector takes fifteen weeks, again broken down into general (nine weeks) and specialized (six weeks) training. The course for inspector takes six months (Ueno 1979: 15; Aichi Prefectural Police 1986: 11). The number of personnel in each rank in Aichi Prefecture are found in table 2.1. As can be seen, there are almost as many sergeants as there are policemen, but the ranks thin out considerably above assistant inspector. The total number of sworn police personnel in 1986 was 11,149 in a prefecture with a population of 6.5 million.

POLICING IN JAPAN

As can be seen in figure 2.3, there are 44 police stations (*keisatsusho*), 368 police boxes (*hashutsusjo,* or *kōban*) and 274 residential police boxes (*chūzaisho*) in Aichi Prefecture. This is typical for prefectures of similar size, and illustrates the fact that police stations do not necessarily coincide with city limits. All police stations come under the jurisdiction of the prefectural police headquarters (*kenkei honbu*), with police boxes coming under the jurisdiction of the appropriate police station. *Kōban* are found in urban areas and *chūzaisho* in rural areas. The former are essentially small offices, with two or three rooms manned by two or three police officers at any given time, while the latter are buildings combining an office with the police officer's (and his family's) living quarters. In urban areas, the police officers report to the appropriate police station to be briefed and then they are dispatched to their individual assignments, including *kōban*. The three-shift system is fairly standard throughout Japan, rotating between routine duty (8:30 A.M. to 5:15 P.M.) the first day, full duty (twenty-four hours, 8:30 A.M. to 8:30 A.M.) the second day, and off on the third day (Ames 1981: 35; Parker 1984: 50; Schembri 1985: 42). The officer is allowed to sleep for up to five hours and is given two hours for meals on the full-duty shift. Most police officers work a total of forty-four hours per week, not counting overtime, which is the standard workweek for all salaried employees in Japan.

Patrol is by foot, bicycle, motorcycle, and car; there are, of course, aerial and marine patrols as well. All officers carry radios, regardless of the means of patrol. As in most countries, the patrolman is the basic unit of law enforcement. The Japanese patrol officer (*qaikin keisatsu*) is usually referred to as "*omawarisan,*" or Mr. Walkaround, even though many police officers these days use bicycles or motorized means of transportation. Central city

Figure 2.3
Organizational Chart of the Aichi Prefectural Police

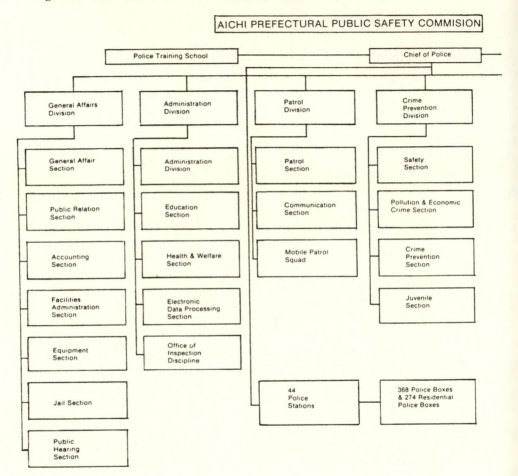

Source: Aichi Prefectural Police 1986, p. 6a.

officers, however, frequently patrol on foot because traffic and narrow roads work against effective motorized patrol. Only the patrolmen from the local *kōban* usually know a neighborhood well. Most streets in Japan do not have names, nor do homes or businesses have addresses as such. Cities are subdivided into "*ku*" or wards, and *ku* are divided into "*cho*" or

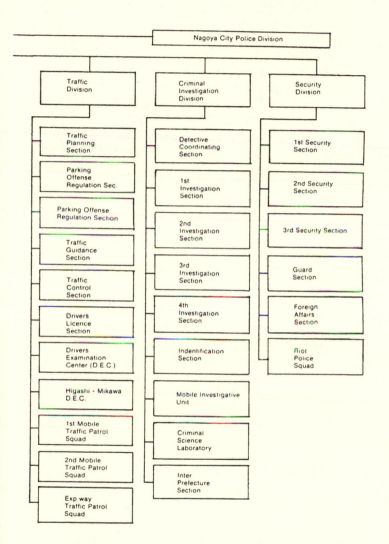

Nagoya City Police Division

Traffic Division	Criminal Investigation Division	Security Division
Traffic Planning Section	Detective Coordinating Section	1st Security Section
Parking Offense Regulation Sec.	1st Investigation Section	2nd Security Section
Parking Offense Regulation Section	2nd Investigation Section	3rd Security Section
Traffic Guidance Section	3rd Investigation Section	Guard Section
Traffic Control Section	4th Investigation Section	Foreign Affairs Section
Drivers Licence Section	Indentification Section	Riot Police Squad
Drivers Examination Center (D.E.C.)	Mobile Investigative Unit	
Higashi - Mikawa D.E.C.	Criminal Science Laboratory	
1st Mobile Traffic Patrol Squad	Inter Prefecture Section	
2nd Mobile Traffic Patrol Squad		
Exp.way Traffic Patrol Squad		

neighborhoods. A *cho* may be further divided into *"chome."* Numbers within the *cho* or *chome* may further designate a location, but not necessarily a specific house or other building. Thus, the police officer must be intimately familiar with his beat. He gains this intimacy through frequent patrol and through twice-yearly household visits (*junkai renraku*). The purpose of these visits is both to get to know every resident or business in the beat through a face-to-face interview and to fill out a Residence Information Card, which contains information on all persons living at that particular residence. These cards are filed at the *kōban* or *chūzaisho* for reference when needed (Ames 1981: 26; Parker 1984: 55-58). Detailed maps for each *ku* or *cho* also designate each house or property by the name of the owner, so that the public can also locate a house.

Police in Japan have a distinctly service, as opposed to law enforcement, orientation. Most of their interaction with citizens deals with noncriminal matters, and the *omawarisan* is usually the first person thought of when a citizen needs assistance of any kind. A breakdown of calls to "110," the nationwide emergency number, shows that only 22 percent of all calls deal with matters that could in any way be considered criminal, and many of them are actually civil in nature; the largest single category of calls (26.3 percent) involves traffic accidents (Parker 1984: 54). *Kōban* often serve as places for citizens to sit and chat with police officers and with each other. As Bayley has stated:

> In order to function successfully as a koban patrolman, one ability above all others needs to be cultivated—the art of patient listening. Policemen spend endless hours allowing people to demonstrate that they are alive, have problems, feelings, values, and a uniqueness that is significant. (1976: 21)

This says a good deal not only about the function of the *kōban* but of the policeman as well. The *kōban* does not serve only as a social meeting place, of course, but as a place for officers to do their paperwork, relax, practice martial arts, and perform housekeeping functions. Except in the smallest *kōban*, there is a resting room separate from the area open to the public, a small kitchen area, and a place to store the bicycles that are used for patrolling (see the diagram in Ames 1081: 36). *Kōban* are easy to find at night because they are identified by a red light or globe.

Kōban patrolmen work closely with neighborhood associations (*chōnaikai*), most of which have an affiliated crime prevention association (*bōhan kyōkai*) or even traffic safety association (*kōtsū anzen kyōkai*). There is usually one home or apartment in each neighborhood designated as a crime prevention checkpoint (*bōhan renrakusho*) that citizens can turn to for assistance and that serves as a direct liaison with the police (Ames 1981: 41-42; Ames 1979: 10; Parker 1984: 176-80). These associations are more than the neighborhood watch programs found in some areas of the United States because the community associations with which they are affiliated are traditional in Japan, well organized, and supported by virtually every home or apartment in the designated geographical area. They serve many more functions as well, participating in the semiannual police crime prevention campaigns, distributing crime prevention literature and advice to all members, and providing tips to police about suspicious activities or people. There are similar associations in rural areas, working closely with the *chūzaisho*. Neighborhoods in Japan are true neighborhoods in that they are geographically defined, are selfsufficient in terms of most needed services, and have a sense of community among their residents.

The neighborhood in which I lived, part of a city of over two million, was just such an area. Directly across the street from my apartment was a market that included a small drugstore, women's apparel shop, and flower shop. Next to the market was a liquor store (with a vending machine that sold not only beer in various sizes and types but also hard liquor when the store was closed), and a few doors away from that was a barber shop. Next to the barber shop was a laundry and photo developing service. Within a block in either direction were numerous small restaurants, bakeries, another market and drugstore, convenience store, magazine shop, and miscellaneous small businesses. There were two hospitals within four blocks in either direction, and the closest *kōban* was approximately eight blocks away. This was typical of most neighborhoods in urban Japan. Combine this sense of community with the many retirees and housewives who devote much of their time to the home, and you have effective crime prevention potential.

Occasionally a community crime prevention association will take on a specific task, such as ridding the neighborhood of *yakuza*. In 1985 in Ebitsuka, a neighborhood of Hamamatsu,[19] a *bōryokudan* called the *Ichiriki Ikka* (One-Power Family) bought a building in a residential area, painted it black, and erected small signs proclaiming it the headquarters of the gang. Although the gang members did not initially threaten members of the community or commit any overt crimes in the community, neighbors were clearly upset with the comings and goings of all of the *yakuza*. The community association erected a two-story portable building on a vacant lot across from the *bōryokudan* headquarters and established a twenty-four-hour watch on them, including videotaping everyone entering or leaving the building. This infuriated the *yakuza*, who started making threats and occasionally brandishing swords in order to intimidate the community association. Ultimately police were assigned to protect the association office, but legally they could do nothing about the *bōryokudan*. The association was not intimidated, however, and further escalated the conflict by hiring a lawyer and obtaining an injunction against the *bōryokudan* activities. Although the lawyer was stabbed and seriously injured by a gang member, the association persisted and ultimately was able to secure substantial restrictions on gang activity, effectively forcing them to move their headquarters elsewhere (*Time* 1988: 42). This was not an isolated incident, only one of the more well-publicized ones. In 1987, 187 offices of *bōryokudan* were ordered removed by courts as a result of civil actions by citizens (*White Paper on Police 1988:* 31).

ORGANIZED CRIME

The incident above illustrates not only the cohesiveness and resolve of community associations but the unusual relationship between the police and organized crime. Organized crime figures are well known in Japan, openly designate their headquarters, and appear frequently in public. They even wear lapel pins bearing their gang's insignia and pass out business cards. Ames (1981: 105) "was struck by the remarkable cordiality between gangsters and the police and the general openness of Japanese gangs." Police officials in fact introduced Ames to top officials of the *Yamaguchi-gumi*, the largest gang in Japan. This is striking to most foreigners, but not to the Japanese who, while not supporting such gangs, tolerate them as long as they do not threaten the daily activities of the citizens (which includes, as in the case cited above, moving into a residential neigborhood).

Bōryokudan derive their income from a variety of sources, some legal and some illegal. The primary illegal sources are blackmail, extortion, drug smuggling and distribution, gambling, and bookmaking. In addition, certain legitimate businesses use *yakuza* for intimidation purposes, such as real estate companies who use gangsters to force tenants out of buildings that the companies desire to sell. *Bōryokudan* also have recently been infiltrating the construction industry, using intimidation to obtain contracts and scare off the competition (Ames 1981: 105). Gang members often have legitimate jobs in addition to working on a more-or-less part-time basis for the gang, and it is estimated that only about one-quarter of gang members earn their income only from illegal sources (ibid.: 116). Some gangs have virtually monopolized certain industries, which they now operate on a legal basis. They have also become much more active as *sōkaiya*, who buy a few shares of a company's stock, attend the annual stockholder's meeting, and create disruptions until they are paid to desist. After this has happened a few times, the mere threat of a disruption is sufficient for a sizable payoff (*White Paper on Police 1988:* 29-31; Ames 1981: 117). It should be obvious, then, that a large amount of illegal *bōryokudan* activity is based upon threats and intimidation; physical violence against innocent citizens is not common, and much *bōryokudan* violence is directed against rival gangs (see the case study in chapter 6). Figure 2.4 shows that on the average one-half of deaths and injuries from firearms in the hands of *bōryokudan* victimize other gang members.

The fact that the three largest gangs have a combined strength of over 31,000, and total membership of all gangs totals over 86,000, shows how difficult it is for the police to effectively combat their activities. It is easier to deal with 86,000 separate criminals than 86,000 organized criminals. And organized they are. The major gangs are highly organized, and the *Yamaguchi-gumi*, with over 21,000 members, even publishes its own magazine. The major gangs have monthly meetings of their top leaders, they issue financial reports, and local affiliates are levied dues to support

Figure 2.4
Situation of Inter-Gang Rivalry Cases and Use of Firearms (1978-1987)

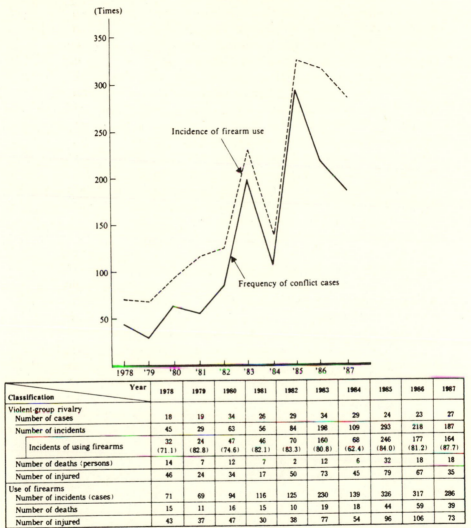

Classification	Year	1978	1979	1980	1981	1982	1983	1984	1985	1986	1987
Violent-group rivalry Number of cases		18	19	34	26	29	34	29	24	23	27
Number of incidents		45	29	63	56	84	198	109	293	218	187
Incidents of using firearms		32 (71.1)	24 (82.8)	47 (74.6)	46 (82.1)	70 (83.3)	160 (80.8)	68 (62.4)	246 (84.0)	177 (81.2)	164 (87.7)
Number of deaths (persons)		14	7	12	7	2	12	6	32	18	18
Number of injured		46	24	34	17	50	73	45	79	67	35
Use of firearms Number of incidents (cases)		71	69	94	116	125	230	139	326	317	286
Number of deaths		15	11	16	15	10	19	18	44	59	39
Number of injured		43	37	47	30	38	77	54	96	106	73

Note: Figures in parentheses are the ratio of use of firearms to the total.

Source: Government of Japan, Naitonal Police Agency, "White Paper on Police 1988"
(excerpt), p. 28.

the national organization (Ames 1981: 118). Until recently the *Yamaguchi-gumi* was run by a group of top leaders, after the assassination of their *oyabun* (or leader) in 1985 (*Newsweek* 1985: 49), but in May 1989 the top leadership finally selected Watanabe Yoshinori, a forty-eight-year-old *yakuza* known for his violence and, interestingly enough, his ability to bring peace to feuding factions. He was formerly the head of the 3,000-member Yamaken gang, based in *Kōbe*, the national headquarters of the *Yamaguchi-gumi* (*The Sunday Star-Bulletin and Advertiser* 5/21/89: E-3). All major gangs now operate with a *oyabun*. Gang members refer to each other by titles derived from familial relationships—"oyabun" means boss or, literally, "parent role"—and in many ways the gangs resemble large families and try to maintain that appearance. They are very tight-knit, and the distinctive feature of many *yakuza* known to those in the West, the missing finger joint, is penance for disloyalty to the *oyabun* or for causing trouble for the gang. Another distinctive feature is the mass of tattoos that adorn many *yakuza* bodies (*Harper's* 1986: 20). These signify toughness (tattooing is painful) and resolve never to leave the gang (such tattoos are stigmas) (Ames 1981: 111).

The difficulty of combatting *bōryokudan* by the police should be obvious, but one method that has achieved a measure of success elsewhere—infiltration or turning of a member—does not seem to be in the arsenal of Japanese police. It is admittedly difficult to infiltrate such a tight-knit organization, especially at higher levels, but available evidence indicates that this is not even attempted by the police. They do, however, make use of electronic eavesdropping (even though this is prohibited under the Constitution), surveillance, and other more traditional forms of law enforcement techniques. Above all, the Japanese police make use of rigorous investigation in all cases involving organized crime, which is folwowed up by vigorous prosecution. The centralized nature of Japanese law enforcement aids in the fight against *bōryokudan*, but the long history and entrenched establishment of organized crime in Japan means that they will very likely always be a part of Japanese society.

ROUTINE POLICE ACTIVITY

Vehicular patrol is not the norm in Japan. In Aichi Prefecture, with a population of almost seven million, and a size of almost two thousand square miles, for example, there are only 1,328 vehicles for patrol, detectives, and other uses, and 1,347 motorcycles, used almost exclusively for traffic enforcement (Aichi Prefectural Police 1986: 13). Most patrol is by foot or bicycle, and is distinctly low-key. Response time varies by degree of urbanization; in Tokyo the average response time for bicycles is under four minutes but for patrol cars it is over five minutes (Allen-Bond 1984: 50), while in more rural areas and smaller cities this pattern is reversed (Ames 1981: 70). Police uniforms are distinctive but not imposing, police vehicles are mid-size Nissans or Toyotas painted black and white, and motorcycles are usually Hondas. Firearms are primarily .38 special Smith & Wesson revolvers or Nambu .38's, although detectives carry .22 caliber weapons.

All weapons are kept in safes at the station when the officers are not on duty. Patrolmen routinely carry batons and are proficient in their use. All police vehicles are equipped with radios and patrolmen carry portable radios with them at all times; communications systems are quite sophisticated.

Japanese police tend, like their American counterparts, to be reactive rather than proactive, and almost exclusively service-oriented. When they do respond to a crime, however, they do so speedily and in force and deal with the crime with great professionalism and thoroughness. Crime scenes are immediately sealed off, detectives and forensic specialists are brought in, and the investigation proceeds smoothly. There does not seem to be the confusion that is often found at crime scenes in the United States, and the order and calm that prevails is notable. Hot pursuit and the capture of a felon, of course, is much the same anywhere, although in Japan only hardened criminals tend to resist the police; the ordinary arrest is a relatively peaceful one. Great care is taken in the investigation of serious crimes. Precise measurements are made, many photographs are taken, witnessess are extensively interviewed, and reports are carefully compiled for presentation to the prosecutor. The police report for the average offense is usually four or five inches thick, and despite its thoroughness the police are frequently asked by the prosecutors for further investigation. After initial investigation of a crime the police have several choices as to disposition of the case, they may forward the investigation report to the prosecutor either with or without arresting the suspect, or they may dispose of the case themselves. The latter procedure, called *bizai-shobun,* may be done in the case of relatively minor offenses such as larceny, fraud, or embezzlement, under criteria established by the local chief public prosecutor. These are cases that the prosecutor feels are not worthy of prosecution even though sufficient evidence exists for prosecution, but the ultimate decision is left to the police. The police must make monthly reports to the prosecutor of cases thus discharged.

As might be expected, Japanese police take particular care in investigating crimes affecting their own. In mid-1989, two police officers in Tokyo were stabbed to death in their *kōban* at about 3 A.M., resulting in a massive manhunt for the killer. It was believed that the man had been brought to the *kōban* for questioning and was able to overpower the officers, although one officer was able to fire several shots at his assailant before collapsing. Witnesses were able to give good descriptions of the killer, who escaped down an alley near the *kōban* (*The Japan Times* 5/17/89: 1). Police officials assigned ninety officers to the case, initially focusing on the knife case and green military gloves left behind by the killer, and ultimately checking a list of 5,000 suspects nationwide as well as going door-to-door in the neighborhood. As of late 1989, the killer was still at large. Such attacks are quite rare; those killed in this incident were two of only sixteen police officers in Japan killed since 1976 (*The Japan Times* 5/20/89: 2).

Detectives (*keiji*) are assigned to specialized sections or divisions much the same way they are in the United States (see figure 2.3). The First Investigative Section of the Criminal Investigation Division in a typical police department handles homicide, robbery, arson, rape, and kidnapping, the Second Section deals with white collar offenses, the Third Section with theft and larceny, and the Fourth with organized crime (J. Crim. Pol. 1985: 5). First Investigative Section detectives also handle industrial accidents resulting in serious injury or death (Ames 1981:132-33), because these are criminal offenses in Japan and may result in criminal sanctions, including incarceration, against those responsible, up to and including company presidents. The actual detective work in Japan, regardless of the type of offense, is much the same as it is in Western nations. There is considerable reliance on informants (*kyōryokusha*, or "cooperators"), and these sources, many of whom are ex-convicts, are carefully cultivated. This cultivation sometimes extends to the detectives assisting the families of those they have arrested (ibid.: 131-32). There is, of course, a good deal of old-fashioned legwork, checking and rechecking of facts and evidence, discussions with fellow detectives, and in general the unglamorous but necessary work that goes into a criminal investigation. Arrests are not usually made until the investigation has been completed, a process that may take weeks or even months, even though the police may have what constitutes probable cause in the United States for an arrest (see the case study at the end of this chapter).

The crime prevention division deals not only with the more obvious types of crime prevention, but with many if not most of those offenses not in the Penal Code, or "special laws." These special laws, discussed in the Preface to this book, involve such offenses as drug abuse, smuggling, weapons, pornography, prostitution, and industrial pollution. This division also handles juvenile cases. Detectives from this section are responsible for supervising businesses that "affect the public morals," such as pornography shops, pachinko parlors,[20] strip shows, and "love hotels" (hotels and motels that rent rooms by the hour for sexual liaisons). They are responsible for carrying out investigations of people who apply for licenses to own rifles or shotguns and also of offenses involving firearms. Citizens are prohibited from possessing handguns in Japan. Swords as well are tightly regulated. A permit is necessary to purchase and keep such a weapon, antique or new, and any violation of these weapons laws would be investigated by Crime Prevention Division detectives. Although pollution cases come under police jurisdiction, only a few are actively investigated, because the police lack both the expertise and the resources to deal with such cases. The political and economic implications of such cases serve as further deterrents to police action (Ames 1981: 138-40).

The traffic division performs the usual functions of traffic police everywhere, although due to the high population density and limited land available for roads and highways they perhaps have a greater burden than many of their colleagues elsewhere. Licensing of drivers in Japan is rigidly controlled. Obtaining a license usually requires successfully completing an approved driving course offered by a commercial driving school, a course that averages two or three hours per day for one month. The written and driving tests are quite difficult, and it is extremely difficult to pass either without having taken a commercial course. The level of competence of Japanese drivers thus tends to be quite high. Nevertheless, there are over 9,000 people killed and over 700,000 injured in traffic accidents in Japan annually, although the rate has been decreasing slightly over the years.[21] Most of the fatal accidents and accidents involving serious injuries are investigated by the police as professional negligence or as gross negligence cases. Driving while intoxicated is a serious offense in Japan, involving not only severe official sanctions but on occasion loss of job as well. Traffic patrols are constantly on the lookout for drunk drivers, and roadblocks by police are not uncommon. There is little excuse for drunk driving in Japan, because the public transportation system is so widespread and efficient that it is not necessary to drive to reach any but the most remote locations, and party-goers who know that alcoholic beverages will be served either take a taxi to the party or designate a driver who does not drink at the party. Public drunkenness, on the other hand, is widespread in Japan, and the after-work drinking ritual is commonplace, as are the large numbers of inebriated businessmen riding home on the subways and in taxis. Most of the serious accidents in Japan, then, are not the result of alcohol but rather of carelessness.

Traffic police have responsibility for all roads and expressways within their area of geographical jurisdiction, although those officers who patrol the expressway system are usually assigned exclusively to that system, and work out of the relevant prefectural police station. The speed limit on the expressways is 100 kilometers per hour, and all vehicles must be equipped with a device that signals the driver when he exceeds that limit—usually a soft chime or buzzer. Radar is used by all traffic police, although for practical purposes it is only effective on expressways and rural highways, because drivers can rarely even attain the posted limit in urban areas except very late at night or early in the morning. Many cars and most taxis have radar detectors. Traffic police make frequent use of the loudspeaker mounted on the roof of their vehicles in warning drivers to obey traffic regulations, warning pedestrians not to jaywalk, or telling bicyclists to stay on the sidewalks. Many people ride bicycles in Japan, and they must share the sidewalk with pedestrians—riding in the street is illegal. All bicycles must be equipped with a bell, and the constant ringing of bells is a common sound on urban sidewalks. Also common are collisions between bicyclists and pedestrians, despite the bells. Many young children riding bicycles wear safety helmets that, although not required by law, are frequently required by parents. Traffic police also stand in intersections and direct traffic. Some of the larger intersections in major cities require several officers to coordinate the large volume of traffic.

The security division of the police department handles subversive groups, provides security for VIPs, and deals with riots and other such disturbances. As might be expected, this work is highly secretive and politically sensitive, and officers assigned to this division do not generally mix with officers from other divisions (Ames 1981: 147). Although both right- and left-wing groups pose dangers to Japanese society, the police tend to pay more attention to groups on the left than on the right, with whom they are more ideologically allied. The targets of much of the work of detectives in this division are radical and terrorist groups who use violence, often in the form of bombs, as part of their efforts to change society, but leftist labor unions and political parties are not immune from security division attention either. In late 1988 an ultra-left group, the *Chūkakuha*, was suspected of having bombed the cars belonging to two Tokyo High Court judges, allegedly because members of the group were being tried for arson by judges living in the compound where the bombings occurred (*The Japan Times* 9/30/88: 3).[22]

Right-wing groups tend to attack those they feel are unpatriotic or against the imperial system, and were suspected in 1987 of having killed a reporter and shooting up the offices of a major newspaper that has been critical of various aspects of Japanese society. Controversy about security officers is not provoked by efforts to prevent such violence, however, but by their surveillance and investigations of legitimate political groups. In 1987, for example, four Kanagawa Prefecture security division police officers were charged with tapping the telephone of the Japan Communist Party's head of international affairs, but were not indicted by the Tokyo District Public Prosecutor's Office despite considerable public and press outcry. The officers allegedly conducted surveillance and wiretapping of, as well as entry into, the party official's home, which was outside of their geographical area of jurisdiction. The police apparently swayed the prosecutors to prevent an indictment. One official in the prosecutor's office said, "Police and prosecutors are like the two wheels of an axle. If the prosecutors indicted the policemen, the police orgnization would become shaky and cooperation between the police and prosecutors in criminal investigations would become difficult" (*The Japan Times* 8/5/87: 2; *Asahi Evening News* 8/5/87: 3). While undoubtedly true, it was perhaps not the most politically acceptable statement that could have been made. It is notable as much for what it says about the power of the prosecutor in Japan as for the relationship between the two groups. The prosecutor also thought that the police officers involved were following the orders of a superior, but inasmuch as the officers would not admit this it was felt that they should not be used as scapegoats.[23]

Police misconduct is handled by the Office of Inspection Discipline of the Administrative Division of the prefectural police department. Most misconduct is in the area of traffic accidents, some of them involving alcohol, although there are occasionally cases of brutality and misuse of weapons, as well as domestic disputes. If the investigation determines that the police officer is guilty of misconduct, he is summarily dismissed, and if the misconduct involves a criminal offense he is immediately arrested as well.[24] There is no right to a hearing, and inasmuch as police in Japan are not unionized, no legal or contractual provisions protect the accused officer. Judging from news reports (or the lack thereof), police misconduct in Japan is relatively rare, and when it does occur it is handled quickly and efficiently. It is likely, of course, that minor cases of misconduct are quietly handled internally, but these cases would not become known to the public. Corruption is virtually nonexistent—there are extremely strong internal pressures and norms that work against corruption at all levels of law enforcement in Japan, and even those most critical of the police for alleged human rights violations generally agree that the police are not corrupt. The constant rotation of senior officers from the NPA to the prefectural level and from the prefectural level to the station level works against the institution of corruption, as does the generally high esteem in which they are held by the public and the general esprit de corps found in the organization.[25]

Japanese police may arrest a suspect under three provisions of the Code of Criminal Procedure. Under Article 199, a police officer (or prosecutor) may request an arrest warrant from a judge after presenting probable cause to that judge and may subsequently make the arrest pursuant to the warrant. Such requests are rarely denied. Article 210 allows the arrest of a person suspected of having committed a serious offense without a warrant if circumstances dictate, but a warrant must be obtained as soon as possible thereafter. Finally, Article 213 allows the arrest without a warrant of a "flagrant offender," defined in the preceding article as a person who could reasonably be suspected of having just committed a crime. Article 203 requires that an arrested suspect be immediately informed of the reason for the arrest and of the right to counsel, and that he must be released or transferred to the prosecutor within forty-eight hours. The suspect may be detained in a police jail for a maximum of twenty-three days prior to indictment. There is no right to counsel during interrogation, although the suspect does have the right to meet with counsel during detention, such access being controlled by the police and/or prosecutor (Article 39, Section 3). In practice, such access is tightly controlled. Meetings generally do not exceed thirty minutes and there are generally less than five meetings during a twenty-three-day detention period. There is no right to bail in Japan, thus making detention decisions significant in terms of freedom for the suspect. The suspect must be warned of the right to remain silent if interrogated, much like the Miranda rule in the United States, a right guaranteed under Article 38 of the Japanese Constitution and legislative acts. Confessions are obtained by the police in over 85 percent of all cases, leading some to believe that the police use coercive techniques, including violence, to extract the confessions (Ames 1981: 136), but there is little evidence of this and the best explanation for the high rate of confessions is cultural.

Police-community relations in Japan seem to be positive, as is the image and status of the police officer. Public opinion polls taken in the 1970s indicate very high satisfaction with *kōban* police officers, with approximately 85 percent of the respondents reporting that they feel friendly or somewhat friendly toward those officers. As might be expected, leftists and scholars have a somewhat less positive attitude about Japanese police (Ames 1981: 181-82). There is also considerable concern about human rights violations by the police. Since 1983, four felony convictions have been overturned due to coerced confessions. In the case of Akabori Masao, the coercion took place in 1954 and he spent thirty-four years on death row before being released by the Shizuoka District Court. Charged with the kidnapping, rape, and murder of a six-year-old girl, he has professed his innocence since the confession was made, a confession he alleges was extracted by physical force. He suffers from a speech impediment and has a history of mental illness, and the court found that his confession lacked credibility, even though they did not find evidence of coercion. He was awarded almost 120,000,000 yen[26] in compensation by the government (Schoenberger 1989: 1, 12-13).

Critics charge that the police keep suspects under constant surveillance, deprive them of sleep and toilet facilities for long periods of time, and coerce them into confessing with promises of release on bail, a hot meal, or the threat that family members may also be arrested (ibid.: 12). Inasmuch as the right to counsel does not adhere until the suspect is charged, and the suspect can be held twenty-three days before being charged, there is considerable time during which coercion, either physical or psychological, can take place. One could argue that the incident cited above occurred over thirty years ago and that those practices are no longer prevalent, but recent press accounts indicate that abuses still exist. The Association of Democratic Lawyers of Japan submitted a report to the United Nations Commission on Human Rights in 1987 alleging the use of torture in two recent cases, and members of the Japan Civil Liberties Union are openly critical of police practices (ibid.). In one of the few reports of Japanese police interrogation by a Western scholar, Ames (1981: 134-35) describes police questioning of a suspected thief, a process which took half a day and utilized the familiar technique of "good buy/bad guy" questioning where one detective is harsh and threatening and the other is sympathetic and understanding. The suspect not only confessed to the crime being investigated but eight other cases as well. The interrogation described by

Ames would not be considered unusual in the United States except that the suspect was not formally arrested and therefore did not have the right to counsel. A case study of a recent crime may illustrate these issues.

Case Study: Kidnapping

This case begins at about 4:15 on a Thursday afternoon in mid-January on a deserted street in a large city in central Japan. A seventeen-year-old high school student was walking home alone when a late model "sporty"-type car drove slowly past her and stopped by the curb ahead of her. A young male got out of the car and asked the girl if he could drive her home. She refused the offer but was grabbed and forced into the car. He locked the car doors from the inside so she could not get out and put the victim's school bag under his seat. The suspect drove aimlessly around the city, refusing her pleas to be released but not threatening her, saying he "wanted to have a relationship with her." After about one hour the victim said that she was thirsty and asked if they could stop so that she could have something to drink. The suspect pulled the car over to the side of the road, saying that he had some drinks in the trunk of the car. He allowed the victim to accompany him to the trunk. She saw three women approaching the car on bicycles and called out to them for help, saying, "Please help me, he took my bag." The women stopped and asked the suspect to return the victim's bag, but he instead got into the car and drove off. The women accompanied the victim to a nearby coffee shop, where she called the police. While she was on the telephone, the suspect returned with the bag and asked her to whom she was talking. When he learned it was the police he ran to his car and drove off. Both the victim and the witnesses were able to describe the suspect and give the license number and description of the car to the police.

The police took a report from the victim and the witnesses, checked the name of the registered owner of the vehicle, and obtained his photograph from driver's license files. They conducted a photo lineup for the victim, and she picked the photo of the suspect from a group of ten photographs. Almost one month after the incident the police, pursuant to a warrant issued by a judge, arrested the suspect. A search of his car revealed a large survival knife wrapped in a cloth on the ledge behind the rear seats of the car (and thus not accessible from the driver's seat), and some condoms. During interrogation of the suspect, with no defense counsel present, the suspect stated that the victim got into the car willingly and denied using any force, although during a later interrogation he admitted the use of force. The police reenacted the offense twice, based on both the victim's statements and the suspect's story, taking numerous photographs and measurements, and drawing a number of diagrams and maps. The police report contained a good deal of personal information about the suspect as well, such as is found in pre-sentence reports in many United States courts.

The suspect was a twenty-three-year-old, fourth-year medical school student[27] from a working class background. He had no prior criminal record but frequented "love hotels." He was charged with violation of Article 220 of the Penal code: "Arrest and Imprisonment. A person who unlawfully arrests or confines another shall be punished with imprisonment at forced labor for not less than three months or more than five years."

The police report that was forwarded to the prosecutor was quite complete, and clearly sufficient for purposes of prosecution. The investigation was thorough, the evidence clear, and the suspect had confessed. The police wanted some sanction levied against the suspect, as did the parents of the victim, who felt that some prison time was warranted. The prosecutor, however, did not feel sufficiently familiar with the suspect to indict at this point, and therefore carried out additional investigation, including further interrogations of the suspect. Particularly troubling was the knife found in the car—was it to be used as a weapon? Was the suspect potentially violent? The prosecutor believed the suspect when he said that he had been given the knife by a fellow student with whom he fished and that he had no intention of using it against the victim, an argument that was supported by the fact that the knife was not accessible to the suspect during the incident and by the statements of the victim that she was not threatened during the ordeal. The prosecutor recommended to the suspect's parents that they hire an attorney, and contacted the parents of the victim to determine whether they would be satisfied with an apology and offering of cash from the suspect. After some persuasion, they said that they would, and the decision was made not to indict the suspect. A profuse apology was made and 100,000 yen offered and accepted. The medical student was strongly encouraged by the prosecutor to sell his car, which he ultimately did.

This incident points out the considerable power of the prosecutor, the topic of chapter 4, but it is also a good example of police investigatory techniques and of the relationship between the police and the prosecutor. While some aspects of this case are unusual, the police approach was typical. Although the police had enough evidence to obtain a warrant under Article 199 of the code of Criminal Procedure as soon as the victim picked the suspect from the photo lineup, they instead waited until more investigation had taken place. They evidently did not feel that the suspect was a threat to society, nor that he would try to flee. Once the arrest had been made, the suspect was subjected to considerable interrogation and required to reenact the crime for the police. Only when the police felt that they had a clear picture of exactly what happened did they forward the by-now voluminous report to the prosecutor.[28] The feelings of the police were clear, but they did not try to influence the decision of the prosecutor in any way.

The prosecutor clearly is above the police in the criminal justice hierarchy, and the police rarely take issue with any prosecutorial decision. A great many police man-hours went into this case, and an outsider cannot help but be impressed with the thoroughness of the police investigation. The report is heavily laden with photographs and diagrams clearly illustrating what took place, and with maps showing the meandering course the suspect took while driving around the city. The fact that the suspect did not drive into the country with the victim was used as evidence that he did not intend to rape her, although it was never clear exactly what his intentions were, and both police and prosecutors felt that the young man had some psychological problems. And yet the substantial police effort in this case did not result in a conviction. Did it result in justice for the victim? For the suspect? Those most directly involved with the case thought that it did for both.

The public remains supportive of the police, and the examples of police abuses publicized are viewed as either aberrations or deserved punishment (Ames 1981: 187-90). Police in any society must by necessity deal with unpleasant events and people, and to maintain order they are empowered and encouraged to restrict certain activities of citizens. Citizens thus affected are likely to harbor resentment toward the police, but citizens who enjoy a low crime rate and the feeling of safety that such a rate provides are likely to credit the police with bringing this about and be willing to put up with some restrictions on their activities in trade. The anomaly in all of this is that vigorous police work has the effect at times of restricting the freedom of certain individuals in society while at the same time increasing the freedom of the society as a whole. People who live in nations with high crime rates tend to forget just how much the threat of crime restricts and shapes our activities, and there is a great sense of freedom and relief in a society like Japan, where the threat of crime is not eminent. The key, of course, is achieving the appropriate balance between effective police work and protection of human rights, and it is not clear whether this balance has been achieved in Japan. What is clear, however, is that the police in Japan are generally viewed favorably by the general population and that in itself is conducive to effective law enforcement. The first chapter of Bayley's pioneering work on Japanese police is titled "Heaven for a Cop," and perhaps that sums it up quite well.

3

Legal Education in Japan

Inasmuch as the subjects of the following chapters—prosecutors, defense attorneys, and judges—all share a common professional education, it is appropriate at this juncture to describe the nature of that education. To understand the nature of their legal education, however, it is necessary to briefly explore Japanese education in general.

The goal of the vast majority of males and an increasing number of females in Japan is a university education at the best university to which the applicant can gain admittance. The "best" university in Japan is Tokyo University, if best is defined in terms of the difficulty of gaining admission and the success of its graduates, with Kyoto University generally considered second. The private universities of Keio and Waseda are probably the top in their category, but are not perceived as being quite the equal of the two national or imperial universities. Virtually all college-bound young people in Japan aspire to attend one of these universities, and they are the ones that produce the bulk of those selected for law study in Japan.

Preparation for admission to top universities in Japan begins at an early age. Education is compulsory through the ninth grade, although the vast majority of students go on to complete high school as well.[29] Preparation for college, however, often begins in preschool. Prestigious (and expensive) preschools are highly sought after; 70 percent of Japanese four-year-olds and 95 percent of the five-year-olds are in preschools (White 1984: 3). As in most countries, all schools are not equal, so conscientious Japanese parents attempt to send their children to the best schools available. Differences between schools are probably considerably less than in the United States, since educational policy is highly centralized in Japan and highly decentralized in the United States, where there is a strong correlation between educational quality and the socioeconomic status of the school district. The Ministry of Education (*Monbusho*) establishes educational policy and standards for all accredited schools, and shares costs with prefectural and local governments. The school year in Japan runs from early April to March of the following year, with a two-month summer break and a short break during the new year period; students attend school 240 days per year (compared to 180 in the United States), attending 5-½ days per week (ibid.). At the end of the twelfth grade, the Japanese student will have almost four American school years more education than his American counterpart (By 1984: 2).

Formal education is only a part of the preparation for college in Japan. The majority of students attend private cram schools, or *juku*, after school and on weekends, and are frequently tutored by their mothers, who consider tutoring one of their primary tasks.[30] The extra work seems to pay off, because there is little doubt that in mathematics and the sciences Japanese education is superior to that of most other countries.

Because high school is not compulsory in Japan, admission is by examination, with competition for the best schools quite heavy. The best schools have the highest percentage of admissions to the top universities, by definition. Many of the top private schools are six-year schools, integrating both junior and senior high. Although almost any student who so desires can get into some high school, only those who score the highest on entrance examinations can get into the most presitigious schools. In order to decide to which high schools to apply, students often take mock entrance exams (*hensachi*) that are supposed to accurately predict true entrance examination success, and even though the Ministry of Education cautions schools against putting too much emphasis on such scores, many junior high school teachers use them for advising purposes. Many of the more prestigious private schools base their curriculum on the university entrance examinations, in effect teaching to the examinations.

All prospective university students in Japan who wish to enter public universities take the same multiple-choice examination in the areas of mathematics, science, economics, geography, history, and English (entrance examinations for private institutions vary considerably). Each university and each school, college, or department within it establishes minimum scores for admission. These scores are generally known by those applying but not officially published or released. Different universities and sub-units within them may establish different scores in each separate area of the standardized examination, such that one institution or department may place more emphasis on mathematics and another on history. All university applicants are notified of their acceptance or rejection on the same day by way of posters bearing their code number (issued by the university upon application) plastered in some prominent spot on the campus to which they have applied. If a code number is not listed, the applicant was rejected. Japanese television annually has scenes of both joyous and grief-stricken students who have seen the results of their examination. There are invariably suicides among the most grief-stricken. Given the implications of gaining admission to the most prestigious institutions, many students who fail to gain admission continue to take the examination and apply year after year until they are finally accepted or until it becomes quite clear that they will never pass. These students are known as *"ronin,"* after the masterless samurai of the Edo period who wandered the countryside seeking a position.

The university curriculum in Japan generally consists of one-and-a-half to two years of general education and two to two-and-a-half years of advanced or specialized instruction. Virtually all of those who want to become lawyers select law as their major (although fewer than half of law majors want to become lawyers). The law curriculum in almost all major universities in Japan revolves around the six codes (the Constitution, Civil Code, Penal Code, Commercial Code, and codes of Civil and Criminal Procedure). There are electives, courses such as the sociology of law or the philosophy of law, but few in comparison to curricula in the United States (Abe 1963: 159-162). Instruction is primarily by lecture and classes tend to be quite large, emphasizing principles and theory rather than practice. The case method is largely unknown, Japan being a civil law nation, and little emphasis is placed on logical reasoning or critical thinking. The goal is to amass large amounts of information. Upon graduation, the student receives a Bachelor of Laws degree (LL.B) or *hōgakushi*, which qualifies a graduate to work in the legal departments of government agencies or private corporations but not to act as a lawyer. To become a lawyer, the graduate must pass the bar exam, or national legal examination (*shihō shiken*) and successfully complete the required course of study at the Legal Training and Research Institute (*Shihō Kenshūsho*). The examination is in three parts, administered several months apart. It is necessary to pass the first part to take the second, and the second to take the third. One may also qualify to take the second part by having completed the general education curriculum of a recognized university (ibid: 566). Most qualify in this manner.

The first examination is not very difficult, consisting of a three-hour multiple-choice test. The multiple-choice questions cover constitutional, civil, and criminal law. The second examination is a difficult essay test administered over a four-day period, covering constitutional, civil, criminal, and commercial law as well as three additional subjects that might include civil or criminal procedure or specialized fields such as criminology, political science, or psychology. Finally, there is an oral examination taken over a one-week period that is generally based on the essay questions (Shikita 1981: 42-43). In 1983, the last year for which figures are available, 25,138 people took the multiple-choice part of the examination and 4,008 of them passed and went on to the essay exam. Only 448 of them passed the last two hurdles, for an overall passage rate of 1.8 percent. The average age of those who passed the examinations and were admitted to the Institute was twenty-eight, indicating that many of the applicants had taken the examinations more than once (the examinations are offered once per year, and there are no limits on the number of times an applicant can take them). In 1983, Waseda Universitgy had the highest number of students entering the Institute (88) with Tokyo (83), Chuo (63), Kyoto (36), and Keio (23) following. Although students from at least fifteen other universities passed the examination, no university was represented by more than 20 students other than those listed above, and most had only 3 or 4 students passing. Tokyo had by far the largest number of students currently enrolled who passed the examinations (32); Waseda, while having the largest representation, had only 5 currently-enrolled students pass (Tanaka 1984: 578).

Where one does one's undergraduate studies is therefore quite important in determining whether one passes the examinations. It is unclear whether this relationship is the result of the highly selective nature of those institutions or the result of superior curricula at those institutions; both factors very likely are involved. Given the role that examinations play in the Japanese educational system, from admittance to high school through the Institute, one might well ask just how valid such examinations are in selecting the best students for the study of law. Validation studies for these examinations such as are done for the Law School Aptitude Test (LSAT) in the United States are not available, but few seriously question the process. The screening process resulting from these series of examinations insures that only a select few ever have the opportunity to become lawyers in Japan, a position with great status but, with few exceptions, unexceptional pay. Lawyers do not fill the ranks of corporate executives or politicians in Japan to anywhere near the extent that they do in the United States, so it is safe to say that those who aspire to the legal profession in Japan do so primarily for reasons other than the opportunity to acquire wealth.

Those admitted to the Institute, about 8 percent of whom are women (*Criminal Justice in Japan* 1983: 46), are called legal apprentices (*shihō shūshūsei*) and receive a basic stipend from the government. The training program consists of an initial four months of classroom training, a sixteen-month internship period, and a final four-month classroom experience, capped off by a final examination. Each incoming group of students is divided into ten classes of approximately fifty each, all of whom receive the same training. The initial four-month curriculum focuses on civil and criminal practice, trials, prosecution, and general culture, and uses a combination of lectures, moot courts, and writing exercises. Instructors consist of full-time staff and part-time lecturers, who utilize materials developed by the Institute rather than standard texts; these materials serve as valuable references to the students after graduation. The students may take a limited number of electives in addition to the required courses (Shikita 1981: 44). The curriculum is intensive and comprehensive, and the students have little time for anything other than study.

The internship phase rotates the apprentices through the three areas of law from which they will select their future profession: private practice, prosecution, and the judiciary. Although the Institute is located in Tokyo, internships take place throughout Japan. Apprentices are assigned to prefectural lawyers' association offices for four months, where they learn the practical aspects of the practice of law and where they assist lawyers in actual cases. In the prosecutorial phase of the internship they are assigned to a district prosecutor's office, where during the four-month experience they learn the powers and procedures of the prosecutor, and under direct supervision of their assigned prosecutor conduct investigations, interview witnesses and suspects, prepare documents, and in general carry out all of the tasks of a prosecutor. They are also assigned for four months each to the civil and criminal divisions of the district courts, where they observe trials, study cases, and participate in judicial deliberations (but not vote) (ibid.). The internship phase of their training not only provides the apprentices with specific substantive and procedural knowledge about various areas of the law, but provides them with information that will be important in the decision that they will have to make upon completion of their training: which of the three areas of law will I enter?

The final four months at the Institute consist of mock trials, discussion of internship experiences, drafting of opinions and generally reinforcing and polishing information previously provided. There are also electives in various specific areas available. Finally, there is an oral and written exmination on the six main subjects covered during the training. Failure is rare. The graduates must then choose between private practice as a lawyer, becoming a prosecutor, or being appointed an assistant judge. To become a prosecutor, one must apply to the Ministry of Justice and go through a personal interview, and to become an assistant judge a similar procedure is followed in the Supreme Court. Those rejected as prosecutors or judges may still become lawyers in private practice. Approximately 75 percent of the graduates become lawyers, while the remaining 25 percent is almost evenly split between those who become prosecutors and those who become assistant judges (Abe 1963: 158). It has been observed that graduates who are policy-oriented opt for prosecution and those with interests in civil law who are more calculated legal thinkers tend to become assistant judges, while most of those choosing to become lawyers are litigators. Older graduates tend to become lawyers, and the trend is toward more graduates selecting private practice (Uchtmann, et al. 1987/88: 357). Although the number of graduates choosing to be prosecutors had been declining, in 1989 fifty-one prosecutors were appointed, the highest number in five years. Six of the fifty-nine were women, and the average age of the newly-appointed prosecutors was 28.4 years (*The Japan Times* 4/5/89: 2). Due to the workload and frequent transfers, however, it is unlikely that a majority of Institute graduates will ever select prosecution over private practice. The legal profession in general, however, continues to be highly attractive to Japanese youth, and is likely to continue to be so given the healthy economic climate in Japan.

It is very difficult to compare education in general and legal education in particular between Japan and the United States. The systems are so different that many comparisons become meaningless. It is possible to make some rather broad generalizations about education in Japan, however, that may shed some light on the nature of the society and of the legal system. It is safe to say that education in Japan has more public support than it does in the United States, and that parents, specifically mothers, spend a good deal more time assisting in the education of their children in Japan than in the United States. This is possible because few Japanese mothers have full-time jobs outside the home. There is virtually no "tracking" in Japanese schools; all students receive basically the same education through the compulsory years. Nor is the quality of education received necessarily based on the affluence of the school district in which one resides, but rather on the school to which one can gain admittance. That, however, may be a function of the private preparatory school the child attends, which in turn may be related to ability to pay. Thus, while the schools themselves do not necessarily produce social stratification, they may reflect that which already exists. Those who are admitted to the Legal Training and Research Institute are, in general, the brightest of those who aspire to a legal education, and represent a rather diverse segment of the population. Unlike the United States, however, there is not a law school for almost everybody who wants to attend one, but only one, and it is highly selective. Does this result in a caliber of legal profession that is distinctly higher than that of the United States? Again, comparisons are difficult, as lawyers in the two countries perform some tasks that are not comparable, but in general it is safe to say that lawyers in Japan are a more elite group than in the United States. One cannot say, however, that this results in a superior legal system. A judgment on that must wait until the system has been examined.

4

Prosecution

Prosecution in Japan is highly centralized, with all prosecutors' offices coming under the Criminal Affairs Bureau of the Ministry of Justice (*Hōmushō*). Unlike the United States, where prosecution is primarily a function of the county and only secondarily a function of the state and federal government, in Japan prefectures and other subdivisions exercise no control whatsoever over prosecution. And although the public prosecutor's office (*kensatsuchō*) is part of the Ministry of Justice and therefore comes under the minister of justice (*hōmu-daijin*), in practice prosecution rests almost entirely in the hands of the prosecutor-general (kenjisōchō), who is appointed by the cabinet. (Public Prosecutor's Office Law, Article 15).[31] Thus, although the minister of justice exercises general policy control over prosecution in Japan, he cannot act with regard to specific cases (PPOL, Article 14).

The prosecutor-general serves not only as the top prosecutor in the country but also as the head of the Supreme Public Prosecutor's Office (*Saikō Kensatsuchō*), which is responsible for all prosecutorial matters at the Supreme Court level. Prosecutors' offices in Japan correspond to the various levels of courts, meaning that there are four levels of prosecutors' offices: supreme, high (*kōtō kensatsuchō*), district (*chihō kensatsuchō*), and local (*kan'i kensatsuchō*). The heads of these offices are called superintending public prosecutors (*kenjichō*) for high public prosecutors' offices, chief prosecutor (*kenjisei*) for district offices, and senior prosecutor (*jōseki kensatsukan*) for local offices. The majority of work takes place at the fifty district prosecutor's offices, which handle virtually all criminal cases (juvenile and adult); high public prosecutors' offices deal only with appeals; and local offices deal with summary court matters. District public prosecutors' offices are usually divided into a general affairs division, which deals with personnel and training matters; an investigation division, which is further broken down into major offenses, security, and traffic sections; and a trial division. Smaller offices, or branches of main offices, may consolidate these functions. Given the nature of prosecution in Japan, the bulk of the work takes place in the investigations divisions.

PERSONNEL

For administrative purposes there are two classes of prosecutors: first and second class. Prosecutors are normally appointed at the second-class level, moving up to first class after having served the required number of years (minimum of eight). Superintending prosecutors and above must be first class prosecutors (PPOL, Articles 15 and 19). As we have seen in chapter 3, graduates of the Legal Training and Research Institute who apply and are accepted are appointed as prosecutors at the second-class level. Others who may be appointed as prosecutors at this level include former judges and professors or assistant professors of law in recognized universities who have at least three years experience (ibid., Article 18). Few prosecutors come from these last two sources. It is also possible for assistant prosecutors (nongraduates of the Institute who assist prosecutors but who do not have the power to indict or appear in court) with three or more years of experience to be appointed second-class prosecutors if they are so recommended and successfully pass the appropriate examination (ibid.). For practical purposes, it usually takes at least seven or eight years as an assistant prosecutor to qualify for such a recommendation. Individuals may also be appointed as first-class prosecutors without having served as a second-class prosecutor if they have been judges for at least eight years or have been judges of the Supreme or High Courts, as may certain categories of other high officials (ibid., Article 19). Such appointments are not common.

Advancement to supervisory positions in the prosecutor's office is almost entirely on the basis of seniority.[32] Prosecutors may be transferred among divisions in the office, and are as a policy transferred to another office every three or four years. One prosecutor I knew had served in four offices during her seven years as a prosecutor, each necessitating a move. Housing is normally provided for the prosecutor, minimizing to some extent the troubles associated with such moves, but transfers are still disruptive.[33] The primary purpose of such transfers is to give the prosecutor a wide variety of experiences, with a secondary purpose being the reduction of the likelihood that dysfunctional relationships will develop between prosecutors and police, judges, or other officials. When a prosecutor has served a sufficient number of years to be considered for a supervisory position, that person will have had a wide variety of assignments in many different prosecutor's offices across Japan.

AUTHORITY

As is the case in the United States, prosecutors in Japan are free to act independently as long as they operate within policy guidelines for their particular office and position. There is little direct supervision, although senior personnel are always available for consultation. Policy guidelines are extensive, ranging from laws passed by the Diet to policies issued on a regular basis from the Ministry of Justice and the Supreme Public Prosecutor's Office. A primary source of both policy guidelines and information on prosecuting is the Prosecution Manual (*Kensatsu Kōgian*) developed by and used at the Institute, a volume used by virtually every prosecutor in Japan. Authority is established by the Public Prosecutor's Office Law (*Kensatasuchō Hō*), which provides in part that "in criminal cases, public prosecutors shall bring public action, request the proper application of law by courts, and supervise the execution of judgments. . . . Public prosecutors may investigate any criminal offense" (Articles 4 and 6).

Further authority and policy is established in the Japanese Code of Criminal Procedure, specifically in Book II, Articles 189 through 270. Articles of particular interest include the following:

Article 191. Prosecutors have the power to conduct independent investigations.

Article 193. Prosecutors have the power to direct police activities relative to specific cases.

Article 194. Prosecutors may file charges against police officials who fail to follow the suggestions and instructions of the prosecutor without good reason.

Article 199. Prosecutors have the power of arrest.

Articles 205 and 208. Prosecutors may request that a suspect be detained up to twenty-eight days.

Article 218. Prosecutors may execute search warrants.

Article 248. Prosecutors may suspend prosecution in the interests of justice.

Article 256. Prosecutors have the power to file an information (indict).

Chapter II of Book II provides that prosecutors may appeal adverse judicial decisions, including sentences. Book VII places in the prosecutor the power and responsibility for executing judicial decisions in criminal cases, including the death penalty, which must be ordered by the minister of justice and observed by both a prosecutor and prosecutor's assistant.

What this adds up to is a considerable amount of legislatively delegated authority. Japanese law provides for specific powers and exercise of discretion that are historical and traditional but not codified in many other countries. There are checks on prosecutorial discretion, but those checks work in a direction opposite from checks in other courties, providing recourse for those who object to a decision *not* to prosecute rather than to a decision *to* prosecute. Policy, whether in the form of legislation or guidelines issued by higher authority, is more likely to expand than to restrict the powers of the prosecutor in Japan, compared to prosecutors in the United States and other Western nations.

PROSECUTORIAL INVESTIGATIONS

It should be stated at the outset that there is no plea bargaining in Japan.[34] The implications of this are many, but initially it means that the charging decision is not influenced by the need for future negotiations with a defense attorney. Before the charging decision is made, however, the prosecutor must conduct an investigation of the case. The case received from the police is normally thoroughly documented, containing not only all details of the alleged offense but of the alleged offender as well. Nevertheless, the prosecutor frequently requests additional investigation from the police. Although Article 192 of the Code of Criminal Procedure states that there shall be mutual cooperation and coordination between the police and the prosecutor, and it is clear that such cooperation and coordination exists, it is also clear that the prosecutor is superior to the police in the criminal justice hierarchy, and that Articles 193 and 194 (see above) more clearly define the relationship than Article 192. As indicated earlier, Japanese police conduct exceedingly thorough investigations. The police report on a case sent to the prosecutor may be one foot thick for an average case, and many feet thick for a major case,[35] but the prosecutors in the investigation division are also very thorough and often want clarification of points they find unclear. Prosecutors frequently go to the scene of an offense so as to get a better idea of what took place, and they usually interview the accused several times.

Article 198 of the Code of Criminal Procedure states that prosecutors "may ask any suspect to appear in their offices and question him" but that the suspect can refuse to appear, must be advised of the right to remain silent, and can refuse to answer questions at any time. Few suspects refuse such a request, however, as the prosecutor in Japan is clearly a symbol of authority not to be challenged. The suspect does not have the right to an attorney during such questioning, and the only other person normally in the room during such questioning is the prosecutor's assistant, who records the interrogation. The interrogation is not only for the purpose of providing additional information for the prosecutor's case but also so that the prosecutor can get a feel for what kind of person the suspect is, information that becomes important when the questions of suspending prosecution or sentence recommendations are considered. The prosecutor may also interview the family of the accused for the same purpose. If the accused has not confessed to the police, the interview by the prosecutor will invariably attempt to obtain such a confession or admission. The prosecutor is barred from offering favorable treatment in return for a confession, but the prosecutor may be more persuasive than the police because the prosecutor can virtually unilaterally determine the disposition of the case. The victim(s) and witnesses are also normally interviewed by the prosecutor, even though they have been previously interviewed by the police and the results of such interviews are included in the police report.[36]

The investigation phase of prosecution is therefore used both for the purposes of determining what evidence is available and for determining the character of the accused. The question arises as to why all of this is necessary, given the fact that the vast majority of cases forwarded by the police contain a confession or admission.[37] The answer is threefold. First, even if there is a confession and the charge is not contested, the case must still be submitted to a judge, who will review the evidence (The Japanese Constitution, Article 38, Section 3, states that nobody shall be convicted solely on the basis of a confession). Second, the investigation is necessary to determine whether there should be a suspension of prosecution. Third, the investigation elicits information necessary in the prosecutor's sentencing recommendation if there is no suspension of prosecution. When there is no confession, the investigation phase is primarily concerned with sufficiency of the evidence, although this accounts for only a little over 13 percent of all cases not prosecuted (see table 4.1).

PROSECUTORIAL DECISION MAKING

At the conclusion of the investigatory phase of the prosecution, several decisions must be made. The first is whether there is sufficient evidence for

Table 4.1
Number of Suspects Not Prosecuted, by Reason (1983-1987)

Year	Total	Suspended of prosecution		Lack or insufficiency of evidence		Non-existence of valid complaint		Lack of mental capacity		Others	
		Number	%	Number	%	Number	%	Number	%	Number	%
1983	115,830	94,235	81.4	14,448	12.5	2,586	2.2	476	0.4	4,085	3.5
1984	107,560	86,655	80.6	13,705	12.7	2,491	2.3	428	0.4	4,281	4.0
1985	97,096	77,661	80.0	12,339	12.7	2,398	2.5	442	0.5	4,256	4.4
1986	93,025	74,643	80.2	12,485	13.4	2,024	2.2	485	0.5	3,388	3.6
1987	98,813	80,093	81.1	13,367	13.5	1,977	2.0	457	0.5	2,919	3.0

Note: Traffic professional negligence and road-traffic violations are not included.

Source: Annual Statistics Report of Prosecution from Government of Japan, Ministry of Justice, Research and Training Institute, "Summary of the White Paper on Crime" (1988), p. 96.

prosecution. In the majority of cases there is. The second decision is what
charge would be appropriate, should there be a decision to indict. The
third, and perhaps most important, is whether prosecution should be
suspended. The charging decision is not difficult, because it is not influenced by plea bargaining considerations nor complicated by various degrees
of offense or detailed elements of the crime. As chapter 1 explains, the
Japanese Penal Code is quite straightforward and definitions of offenses are
rather simple compared to those in the most United States jurisdictions.
And it is extremely rare, as we shall see, for a Japanese defense attorney to
quibble over whether his client committed all elements of the offense charged.
The important decision, then, is whether to indict (*kiso suru*), or to state it
another way, whether to suspend prosecution (*kiso yūyo*).

As we can see from tables 4.2 and 4.3, a significant number of prosecutions
are suspended, and the trend is increasing.[38] The overall rate of 17 percent
in 1987 is defined as the number of suspects granted suspension divided by
those prosecuted and granted suspension (*White Paper on Crime 1888*: 15).
Suspensions of prosecution as a percentage of all dispostions in 1987 constituted 13.5 percent[39] (ibid.: 13). Thus, a substantial number of offenders
against whom there was sufficient evidence to prosecute were not
prosecuted.[40] As may be seen in tables 4.2 and 4.3, this decision varied considerably by offense, ranging from high rates for larceny and gambling to
low rates for homicide and stimulant drug offenses (excluding traffic
cases).[41] Prosecution of crimes of violence is not suspended as frequently as
crimes against property, but drug offenses, which do not involve a victim,
are treated more severely than rape or robbery. As might be expected,
members of organized crime gangs were treated with somewhat less leniency
than the rest of the criminal population, although certain offenses, such as
unlawful assembly with a weapon, were exceptions (see table 4.4). It is interesting to note that certain offenses are not listed in these tables, among
them crimes involving public officials. One such crime is "abuse of authority"
(Penal Code, Articles 193 and 194), which is listed in a separate table by the
Ministry of Justice and which includes only the number of cases disposed of
by prosecutors and the prosecution rate in a given year. Although the
number of cases usually runs over 1,000 per year (1987 was an exception
with only 486), the prosecution rate is quite low, ranging from 0 in 1985
through 1988 to .3 in 1984. Dando (1970: 525) indicates that this might be
the result of bias on the part of prosecutors.

Article 248 of the Code of Criminal Procedure is quite specific in the
factors that may be considered when suspension of prosecution is to be
considered:

If, after considering the character, age, and situation of the offender, the gravity of
the offense, the circumstances under which the offense was committed, and the conditions subsequent to the commission of the offense, prosecution is deemed
unnecessary, prosecution need not be instituted.

Table 4.2
Number of Suspects Disposed of by the Public Prosecutor's Office,
by Offense (1987)

Offence	Total	Prosecution		Non-prosecution		Referral to family court
		Formal trial	Summary proceedings	Suspension of prosecution	Others	
Total	2,647,253	125,421	1,617,087	356,283	51,622	496,840
Penal Code offences	933,272	79,730	297,674	266,535	42,135	247,198
Homicide	2,868	1,060	—	57	1,667	84
Robbery	1,753	872	—	53	240	588
Bodily injury	30,566	4,856	11,003	3,639	751	10,317
Assault	7,824	390	3,707	2,043	82	1,602
Extortion	11,454	3,743	—	1,375	426	5,910
Larceny	205,107	37,513	—	30,067	2,853	134,674
Fraud	17,573	10,095	—	4,237	2,429	812
Embezzlement	26,613	1,323	91	4,159	475	20,565
Rape	1,902	803	—	161	360	578
Indecent assault	1,314	437	—	76	399	402
Public indecency	910	38	640	155	6	71
Distribution of obscene literature, etc.	1,066	528	335	165	23	15
Arson	1,080	580	2	118	246	134
Bribery	682	460	57	107	58	—
Gambling	7,473	1,723	3,061	2,446	81	162
Violent acts	5,688	1,039	1,471	567	140	2,471
Traffic professional negligence	584,905	9,825	272,593	211,839	27,315	63,333
Others	24,494	4,445	4,714	5,271	4,584	5,480
Special Law offences	1,713,981	45,691	1,319,413	89,748	9,487	249,642
Firearms and swords	4,839	1,482	1,768	927	223	439
Stimulant drugs	27,273	22,858	—	1,302	1,547	1,566
Road-traffic violations	1,578,642	10,725	1,271,595	64,351	5,587	226,384
Others	103,227	10,626	46,050	23,168	2,130	21,253

Source: Annual Statistics Report of Prosecution from Government of Japan, Ministry of
Justice, Research and Training Institute, "Summary of the White Paper on Crime"
(1988), p. 14.

It should be noted that the Penal Code does not refer to "suspension of
prosecution." The term is somewhat misleading, because prosecution in
such cases is, in a practical sense, terminated, not suspended to be instituted
again should circumstances warrant. The code also does not tell the
prosecutor how much weight should be given to each factor, nor how to interpret the "circumstances" of the offense or the "conditions subsequent" to

Table 4.3

Rate of Prosecution and Suspended Prosecution, by Offense (1985-1987)

Offence	1985		1986		1987	
	Prosecu-tion rate	Suspen-tion rate	Prosecu-tion rate	Suspen-tion rate	Prosecu-tion rate	Suspen-tion rate
Total	89.8	8.4	89.0	9.2	81.0	17.0
Penal Code offences (excluding traffic professional negligence)	60.1	34.4	59.5	34.8	57.7	36.5
Homicide	65.7	5.4	58.1	4.9	38.1	5.1
Robbery	78.7	7.0	73.8	8.8	74.8	5.7
Bodily injury	83.0	14.5	82.7	14.1	78.3	18.7
Extortion	66.8	26.6	68.2	26.1	67.5	26.9
Larceny	54.1	43.8	54.5	43.5	53.3	44.5
Fraud	64.0	28.7	60.7	31.7	60.2	29.6
Rape	63.0	14.5	62.4	13.9	60.6	16.7
Indecent assault	46.1	14.6	50.0	12.4	47.9	14.8
Arson	64.5	15.5	60.3	15.5	61.5	16.9
Bribery	72.5	21.5	70.5	24.2	75.8	17.1
Gambling	74.7	24.4	68.6	30.6	65.4	33.8
Violent acts	80.6	17.2	79.1	18.6	78.0	18.4
Traffic professional negligence	73.0	22.4	72.8	23.0	54.1	42.9
Special Law offences (excluding road-traffic violations)	79.2	17.9	78.1	19.3	73.9	23.5
Firearms and swords	74.4	21.8	76.3	20.0	73.9	22.2
Stimulant drugs	89.1	5.5	89.5	5.2	88.9	5.4
Road-traffic violations	97.0	2.7	96.5	3.2	94.8	4.8

Note: Suspension rate = $\dfrac{\text{number of suspects granted suspension}}{\text{number of suspects prosecuted and granted suspension}} \times 100$

Source: Annual Statistics Report of Prosecution from Government of Japan, Ministry of Justice, Research and Training Institute, "Summary of the White Paper on Crime" (1988), p. 15.

the offense, although there is general policy on such matters in prosecutors' offices. "Conditions subsequent to the commission of the offense" generally refers to apology and restitution or cash offering on the part of the offender and forgiveness on the part of the victim and/or family of the victim, as was illustrated in the case study in chapter 2. "Circumstances of the offense" deals primarily with the use of excessive force or cruelty during the commission of a crime. The weighting factor, however, is discretionary on the part of the prosecutor.

Unfortunately, little empirical research has been done on factors relating to the suspension of prosecution. The only known study, available only in Japanese, was done by Mitsui Makoto in 1974 and concerned larceny and assault cases dealt with by a summary court in 1967 and 1968. Most of his

Table 4.4

Number and Percentage of Prosecutions and Suspended Prosecutions for
Bōryokudan Members, by Offense (1987)

Offence	Prosecution		Non-prosecution		Percentage of prosecution	Percentage of suspended prosecution	Total disposition	
	Total	Formal trial	Total	Suspension			Percentage of prosecution	Percentage of suspended prosecution
Total	13,704	10,668	2,977	1,936	82.2 (77.8)	12.4	64.3 (59.0)	31.1
Penal Code offences	8,539	6,122	2,186	1,555	79.6 (71.7)	15.4	57.7 (73.6)	36.5
Homicide	253	253	43	4	85.5 (100.0)	1.6	38.1 (100.0)	5.1
Bodily injury	2,634	1,642	259	194	91.0 (62.3)	6.9	78.3 (30.6)	18.7
Assault	579	141	65	59	89.9 (24.4)	9.2	65.8 (9.5)	33.3
Extortion	1,604	1,604	653	484	71.1 (100.0)	23.2	67.5 (100.0)	26.9
Unlawful assembly with weapon	48	35	62	46	43.6 (72.9)	48.9	37.0 (68.3)	57.7
Larceny	452	452	144	127	75.8 (100.0)	21.9	53.3 (100.0)	44.5
Gambling	622	409	117	83	84.2 (65.8)	11.8	65.4 (36.0)	33.8
Violent acts	960	517	250	186	79.3 (53.9)	16.2	78.0 (41.4)	18.4
Others	1,387	1,069	593	372	70.1 (77.1)	21.1	52.2 (77.1)	36.2
Special Law offences	5,165	4,546	791	381	86.7 (88.0)	6.9	73.9 (42.2)	23.5
Firearms and swords	796	718	157	74	83.5 (90.2)	8.5	73.9 (45.6)	22.2
Stimulant drugs	3,186	3,186	392	113	89.0 (100.0)	3.4	88.9 (100.0)	5.4
Anti-prostitution law	129	103	13	12	90.8 (79.8)	8.5	84.4 (59.3)	14.9
Horse Race Law	150	112	12	4	92.6 (74.7)	2.6	90.6 (22.2)	8.4
Bicycle Race Law	32	27	1	—	97.0 (84.4)	—	90.5 (28.2)	8.5
Others	872	400	216	178	80.1 (45.9)	17.0	67.9 (16.5)	30.2

Notes: 1. Traffic professional negligence and road traffic violations are excluded.

2. Percentage of prosecution $= \dfrac{\text{prosecution}}{\text{prosecution} + \text{nonprosecution}} \times 100$

3. Percentage of suspended prosecution $= \dfrac{\text{suspended prosecution}}{\text{prosecution} + \text{suspended prosecution}} \times 100$

4. Percentage of formal trial $= \dfrac{\text{formal trial}}{\text{prosecution}} \times 100$

5. Figures in parentheses show the percentage going to formal trial among those prosecuted.

Source: Annual Statistics Report of Prosecution and Statistics Report of Prosecution (Offenses Related to *Bōryokudan*) from Government of Japan, Ministry of Justice, Research and Training Institute, "Summary of the White Paper on Crime" (1988), p. 72.

findings are as expected: suspension of prosecution in larceny cases is more likely to take place if the method of the crime is not aggressive (i.e., shop-lifting versus forceful entry), in cases where the offender was young and had no prior record, where the goods were recovered, where the goods were of lesser value, where the victim forgave the offender, where the offender's family or employer took responsibility, and where the police requested lenient treatment (Mitsui 1974: 1713-16). Similar results were found in assault with bodily injury cases, although here several additional factors were added, such as the offender's education, whether the offender was a *yakuza* or not, the nature of the injury to the victim, and the relative culpability of the victim. Generally, the higher the education of the offender the more likely prosecution would be suspended, the more serious the injury the less likely was suspension, and the more culpable the victim the more likely suspension. If the offender was a *yakuza*, suspension of prosecution was highly unlikely (ibid.: 1723). Mitsui was concerned that emphasis on rehabilitating offenders might be greater than emphasis on the general prevention of crime, and that such emphasis could threaten the individuals' rights of privacy as a result of the detailed investigation into their personal histories. He concludes that prosecutors emphasize rehabilitative factors over general deterrent factors (ibid.: 1736-38).

While the Mitsui study is significant if only for the fact that it is unique, it has limited applicability today. The data are old and the study examined only a summary court in one jurisdiction and is therefore of questionable application to the nation as a whole. There is little doubt, however, that the factors Mitsui identifies play a major role in suspension of prosecution deci-sions. A method of validation of these findings as well as a means of further understanding prosecutorial decision making is the examination of case studies. Goodman (1986) has case studies from the Tokyo District Prosecutor's Office that allow some insight into the decision-making process. Two of the cases involved the death of infants, one as a result of negligence and the other by design. In the first case, the infant was smothered by a stack of newspapers that fell on him when his mother momentarily left the house. The prosecutor decided to indict under Article 210 of the Penal Code, "Causing Death through Negligence," because he felt that such negligence was inexcusable. The statutory penalty for this offense is a fine of not more than 1,000 yen.[42] The prosecutor was overruled by his superior, who felt that the loss of the child was sufficient punishment, that the woman would not allow such a thing to happen again, and punishment, however mild, would be cruel (Goodman 1986: 38-39). The second case involved a mother's impulsive killing of a deformed child (her second such child). Although she clearly intended to kill the child, she had an IQ below normal and her husband and his family did not want prosecution. Taking these factors into consideration, the prosecutor decided to suspend prosecu-tion. Fellow prosecutors thought that a suspended sentence was more ap-propriate, as suspension of prosecution was unusual in such cases and the prosecutor should not be in a position of giving sanction to infanticide (ibid.: 39). An infanticide case occurring in 1988 might be valuable to examine at this point.

Case Study: Infanticide

At about noon on February 10, 1988, the accused called her brother from their parents' house to tell him that her three-month-old son was not moving. The brother immediately went to the house and took the apparently lifeless child and its mother to the hospital, where the child was declared dead. The hospital personnel noticed marks around the child's neck and discovered from the mother that she had strangled the child. The police were called and took the woman to the police station for questioning. Her husband was also notified and met her there. She again admitted that she had strangled the child, saying that she had to do it to "lift the heavy burden on her." A warrant was obtained and the woman was formally arrested. The investigation revealed that the twenty-seven-year-old woman had a low IQ, barely graduated from junior high school, and had not been able to keep a responsible job for very long. At the time of the crime, she was employed at a copy center making xerographic copies for about 100,000 yen per month. Her parents had opposed her getting married and having children because they felt that she was not intelligent enough to handle either responsibility, but she became pregnant and her parents relented. She was married in May 1987, and the child was born in October. She had not wanted children but her husband did and she was obedient. He realized that she would have a difficult time due to her limited intelligence and dislike of children, but he was willing to give up his job as a taxi driver and take a lower-paying job that would allow him to spend more time at home with the child. Even this was not enough, however, and the accused's parents had to assist in caring for the child, because the mother simply did not want to feed or otherwise care for the infant.

Beginning in December 1987, the accused made several unsuccessful attempts to kill herself and the child. She made superficial cuts on her wrists on one occasion and a half-hearted effort to strangle the child, and on another she swallowed a needle and tried to smother the child. On yet another occasion she turned on the gas in the apartment but turned it off after about ten minutes. The police suggested that her husband take her to a hospital for a psychiatric evaluation after the gas incident, but she refused to talk to the psychiatrist. At this point her husband moved the family to her parents' home, where he thought she might have more supervision, even though both parents worked. The incident in question occurred while the parents were at work. Although the police report contained most of the information cited above, the prosecutor interviewed the accused's parents and husband at length in order to determine the motive for the crime as well as to obtain the complete history of the accused. The prosecutor further referred the woman for a psychiatric evaluation, which revealed her to be sane, with an IQ of 59, and able to communicate on a very basic level.

The prosecutor considered all of the factors and decided to indict. The crime was a serious one but there were mitigating circumstances. The husband was seeking a divorce but did not want the woman imprisoned; she did not want to remarry because she realized that she could not handle the responsibility. Her parents promised to care for her once the case was settled. The prosecutor felt, however, that the tragedy was avoidable, as there was more than sufficient warning that it might occur, and that imprisonment would serve as a message to others that such warnings should be heeded. The minimum penalty in such a case (Article 199, homicide) is three years, and that term was recommended by the prosecutor in charge of investigation. The prosecutor's immediate superior felt that four years would be more appropriate due to the age of the child; had the child been younger he would not have had as "strong a desire to live." Both prosecutors agreed that had the woman been of normal intelligence a term of six or seven years would have been appropriate. In the end, after discussion with the trial prosecutor, it was decided that a recommendation of five years imprisonment would be made. The prosecutor predicted, however, that the judge would sentence her to three years imprisonment with a five-year suspension of execution of sentence (under Article 25 of the Penal Code), which the prosecutor thought was appropriate but which could not be officially recommended due to the seriousness of the crime. During the trial, the ex-husband testified on her behalf, asking the judge not to sentence her to prison. The sentence was exactly as predicted. Neither side appealed.

There are similarities to the case described by Goodman and there are differences. Neither woman was imprisoned, but a sentence of three years suspended for five years is clearly more severe than a suspended prosecution. Infanticide is not uncommon in Japan, but it is usually accompanied by the suicide of the mother. It is more acceptable in Japan to kill one's child or children with ones' self than to kill ones' self and spare the child or children, leaving them motherless. The type of infanticide found in these two cases is different, however.

Despite the mitigating circumstances of low intelligence, some punishment is warranted in the minds of most prosecutors. Mitsui's thesis seems to be supported in one of these cases but not the other. In the case related by Goodman, the rehabilitation factor seemed to be paramount, while in the second case the general deterrence factor weighed more heavily. The second case also illustrated an interesting approach to the law on the part of the prosecutor's office, in that the official prosecutorial sentence recommendation was not necessarily what was desired by the prosecutor nor what the prosecutor felt would be imposed, but one that was intended to send a message to the public. In other cases prosecutorial sentence recommendations are intended to be followed and usually are. This type of case is unusual, however, and calls for an unusual approach to sentencing.

Although these factors characteristically play a major role in the suspension of prosecution decision, there is another important factor which is uniquely Japanese. One of the considerations stated in Article 248 is "conditions subsequent to the commission of the offense," which involves the relationship between the offender and victim (or victim's family). This relationship has to do with remorse on the part of the offender, apology and/or a settlement with the victim, and the feelings of the victim about the offender (Shikita 1980: 6). In the case study found in chapter 2, the offender's attorney suggested that the offender personally apologize and offer a cash settlement to the victim and her family. While it is difficult to place a cash value on an offense not involving property or bodily injury, there are generally accepted figures in such cases that are felt to be adequate. The primary value of such an offering is, of course, symbolic, but that symbolic gesture combined with an apology given in the humble form of address in Japanese is usually sufficient to convince the victim(s) that the offender is sincerely remorseful and therefore deserving of leniency. In the kidnapping case, both the victim and her parents initially wanted the offender to be incarcerated, and both the prosecutor and defense attorney tried to convince them that incarceration might not be appropriate in such a case. The selling of the car on the part of the offender was also a symbolic gesture designed to show remorse and, according to the prosecutor handling this case, was difficult to bring about, as the prosecutor had no legal authority to order such an act. Financial settlements and other such symbolic acts in criminal cases may seem unusual to the Western eye, but are not only quite common but expected in Japan.

Apology plays a very important role in Japan, but the use of apology is significantly different than its use in Western societies. In Japan, for example, one rarely apologizes when bumping into others in a crowded subway or on the street but apologizes profusely for minor transgressions involving those one knows personally. The key factor here is the difference between the in-group and the out-group, for in Japan relationships within the in-group are all-important while relations between out-groups are usually marked by indifference or even slight hostility (Wagatsuma and Rosett 1986: 465). Victims and offenders are not usually members of the same group, and therefore their relationship is formally an out-group relationship, but their relationship as offender and victim changes the equation such that in-group norms apply to them. Apology is therefore called for. Apology may take the form of a face-to-face encounter or a letter of apology (shimatsusho) or both, and is almost always accompanied by a symbolic cash offering.[43]

One test of the efficacy of suspension of prosecution as a rehabilitative tool is the amount of recidivism of those given such treatment. Again, however, we have very little empirical evidence on which to base an opinion. The only study available (reported by Dando 1970: 527-28) is based on a sample of 9,296 cases out of a total of 246,000 in 1964 in which suspension of prosecution was granted. Although the overall recidivism rate was slightly over 13 percent, the rate varied considerably depending upon the offense. The rate for fraud, for example, was 33.3 percent and for crimes of violence, 15.5 percent (ibid.). Overall recidivism rates in Japan are also difficult to come by, but some figures are useful. In 1987, 60 percent of all newly admitted prisoners had previously served time in prison (*White Paper on Crime 1988:* 113), while in the same year the recidivism rate for adult parolees was 1.5 percent and for adult probationers it was 33.2 percent (ibid.: 125). There are clearly methodological problems in the survey reported by Dando, and it is unfortunate that more comprehensive studies of recidivism among those given suspension of prosecution have not been conducted. Criminal records in Japan are largely computerized and while this aids the prosecutor in making decisions regarding prosecution, it also enables research on recidivism to be done quite easily. Personal impressions among some prosecutors indicate that recidivism is highest among those who commit offenses involving theft, fraud, and drugs, but again this is not based on empirical studies but rather on years of experience. Shikita (1980: 8) indicates that suspension of prosecution is not controversial in Japan due to confidence in the prosecutor as an institution and due to the fact that such decisions must be approved by a superior. Shikita (a former prosecutor) stated that, based on his experience, 60 percent to 70 percent of such decisions are approved without modification.

It is likely that not all victims will agree that suspension of prosecution is in the best interests of justice. Such victims have recourse under Japanese law through two mechanisms: inquest of prosecution (*kensatsu shinsakai*) under the Inquest of Prosecution Law (*Kensatsu Shinsakai Hō*), and analogical institution of prosecution (*saibanjō junkiso tetsuzuki*) under Articles 262-269 of the Code of Criminal Procecure. Under the first mechanism, inquest of prosecution, a victim or complainant who feels that prosecution was improperly suspended or declined may take the case to a local commission consisting of eleven citizens who serve six-month terms. The commission is attached to, but not under the direction of, the local district court, and may conduct an independent investigation of the circumstances surrounding the case and the decision not to prosecute (Suzuki 1980: 13). Eight of the eleven members must approve a recommendation that prosecution be initiated (George 1984: 64-65). The commission has only advisory power, although by law the chief prosecutor of the district prosecutor's office in question must review the case. As tables 4.5 and 4.6 illustrate, there are relatively few such cases referred each year, and of those only a small number result in prosecution. Chief prosecutors clearly disagree with most recommendations, and given the fact that the commission consists of laypeople, it is quite likely that different considerations prevail for the commission and the prosecutor. Opinion is split between those who advocate abolition of the system as expensive and

Table 4.5
Reception and Disposition of Cases Applied to the Inquest of Prosecution
(1982-1986)

Year	Cases newly received			Cases disposed				Un-decided
	Total	Complaint	Ex-officio application	Total	Propriety of prosecution·Impropriety of non-prosecution	Propriety of non-prosecution	Others	
1982	3,091	2,896	195	2,724	93	2,268	363	1,788
1983	1,971	1,743	228	2,524	64	2,187	273	1,235
1984	1,405	1,161	244	1,620	57	1,292	271	1,020
1985	2,244	2,067	177	1,579	58	1,232	289	1,685
1986	1,248	1,034	214	2,364	44	2,037	283	569

Source: Criminal Division of Supreme Court from Government of Japan, Ministry of Justice,
Research and Training Institute, "Summary of the White Paper on Crime" (1988),
p. 104.

ineffective and those who would make the commissions' decisions binding
(Dando 1970: 531).

The second avenue of recourse, analogical institution of prosecution, is
used less frequently and with less success. This procedure is designed to deal
with nonprosecution of cases involving abuse of authority by public

Table 4.6
Post-Disposition of Cases Decided as Propriety of Prosecution/Impropriety
of Nonprosecution, by Grounds of Former Nonprosecution Decision
(1982-1986)

Year	Total			Suspension of prosecution				Insufficiency of suspicion				Others			
	Prosecution	Support of non-prosecution	Rate of prosecution	Sub-total	Prosecution	Support of non-prosecution	Rate of prosecution	Sub-total	Prosecution	Support of non-prosecution	Rate of prosecution	Sub-total	Prosecution	Support of non-prosecution	Rate of prosecution
1982	90	8	82	8.9	13	—	13	—	76	8	68	10.5	1	—	1	—
1983	97	7	90	7.2	8	1	7	12.5	89	6	83	6.7	—	—	—	—
1984	68	8	60	11.8	8	1	7	12.5	59	7	52	11.9	1	—	1	—
1985	49	15	34	30.6	7	4	3	57.1	41	11	30	26.8	1	—	1	—
1986	51	14	37	27.5	16	8	8	50.0	34	6	28	17.6	1	—	1	—

Source: Criminal Division of Supreme Court from Government of Japan, Ministry of Justice,
Research and Training Institute, "Summary of the White Paper on Crime" (1988),
p. 105.

officials, which we have seen has a very high rate of suspension of prosecution. The aggrieved party must first request in writing that prosecution take place, and if prosecution is declined, the party may apply to the district court having jurisdiction in the case. First application must take place within seven days of notification of nonprosecution. A three-judge panel will then investigate the claim and rule either for or against prosecution, with prosecution being conducted by a private attorney appointed by the court (Articles 260-267, Code of Criminal Procedure). From 1982 to 1986 only two cases were ordered prosecuted out of 3,574 requests (*White Paper on Crime 1988:* 105). While it may seem that this system has very little value, some scholars believe that its primary significance is as a deterrent to prosecutors who might be tempted to not prosecute a public official (Dando 1970: 529; George 1984: 68). Because the appeal must be in writing and must be presented to the chief prosecutor and then to a court, the process very likely serves as a deterrent to those who feel that they have been done an injustice, and may well explain why the inquest of prosecution option is more frequently used.

Article 40 of the Japanese Constitution says that any person who has been arrested and detained and is subsequently acquitted may sue the State for redress as provided by law (the Criminal Compensation Law—*Keiji Hoshō Hō*). The law does not cover, however, those who were investigated and charged without having been arrested or detained, nor does it cover those who were arrested or detained but never prosecuted (See George 1984: 61-62). Such compensation is not easily obtained, as a case decided by the Supreme Court in 1989 illustrates. In 1974, Masaru Matsunaga was convicted of murdering a police officer during a violent strike in Okinawa in 1971. His conviction was overturned in 1976 by a high court, after which Matsunaga sued for compensation and was awarded 3.5 million yen in 1983 by the Tokyo High Court, which found that his indictment was illegal. The case was appealed to the Supreme Court, which ruled that the High Court had not adequately determined whether the prosecutor's actions were fair and returned the case to that court for further proceedings (*The Japan Times* 6/30/89: 2).

The Ministry of Justice has issued an order titled "The Regulation for Suspect Compensation" (*Higisha Hoshō Kitei*), which allows a prosecutor to recommend compensation for a suspect who has been arrested or detained but who, in the prosecutor's opinion, did not commit an offense. The suspect must request such compensation and the amount of compensation is made part of the prosecutor's recommendation. Articles 188-2 through 188-7 of the Code of Criminal Procedure provide for indemnification by the government for the costs of a trial where the defendant was found not guilty. The party must request such compensation from the court rendering the not guilty verdict, and, should compensation be made, it covers not only attorney fees but also travel expenses and per diem. If the prosecution appeals the verdict and the original verdict is upheld, the ex-defendant may also request compensation for costs associated with the appeal. In 1986, sixty-two people who were detained for a total of 45,112 days (for an average of 70.5 days each) and later found not guilty were awarded a total of 289,320,400 yen, or an average of 6,413 yen for each day of detention (*White Paper on Crime 1988*: 104). These procedures not only provide avenues of recourse for those accused but not convicted, but act as deterrents to prosecutors who might be tempted to indict on scanty evidence.

PROSECUTION

If the prosecutor decides to indict, an information is filed. There is no grand jury system in Japan. Following the indictment, a choice must be made between summary procedure (*ryakushiki tetsuzuki*) and a regular trial. If the defendant agrees to a summary procedure, the prosecutor sends the evidence in the case, the defendant's consent form, and a penalty recommendation to the judge; no appearance is necessary (Araki 1985: 619). Normally, the summary court (*Kan'i Saibansho*) can only impose a fine, but in exceptional cases it may sentence a defendant to a maximum of three years. In 1986, 93 percent of all prosecutions were handled through summary proceedings, while over 99 percent of all cases adjudicated by summary courts made use of the summary proceedings (*White Paper on Crime 1988:* 14, 97). The advantage of the summary procedure, to both prosecutor and defendant, is speed, as the case can be disposed of quite quickly using this method. If the defendant has confessed and is satisfied with the proposed sentence recommendation of the prosecutor, there is no need to appear in court. There are, however, due process issues involved in this procedure that would prevent its use in the United States, primary among them being the absence of a judge to inform the defendant of his or her rights. The quasi-magisterial role of the prosecutor is accepted in Japan, and few question the ability of the prosecutor to fully inform the defendant of his or her rights and of the implications of opting for the summary procedure rather than a formal trial, but the potential for abuse remains nevertheless.

Where the defendant contests the charge or the sentence recommendation, or where the defendant does not want the case heard by summary procedure, the case will go to trial in the appropirate summary court to be heard by a single judge or to the district court to be heard either by a single judge or by a three-judge panel, depending upon the seriousness of the offense. There are two types of trials: the modified public trial procedure (*kan'i kōhan tetsuzuki*) and the regular trial procedure. The former procedure, to be used only when the charge is not a serious one and is not contested, simplifies procedures in the interest of speed and places great reliance on the prosecutor's written case. Most cases heard in the summary court (but not using summary procedures) use this method, while it is much less frequently used in the district courts (Araki 1985: 622). Prosecutors from the district public prosecutor's office trial division argue cases in these courts. As chapter 6 explains, the trial procedure is different in many respects from felony criminal trials in the United States. The state has the burden of proof, as in the United States, but the Japanese rely more on documentary evidence and less on testimony. Thus, the primary job of the prosecutor is to prepare the documents to be submitted to the court and to answer any questions regarding them from the judge(s). The oral skills required in the American courtroom are generally unnecessary in Japan, both because there is no jury to convince in Japan and because the Japanese system places more emphasis on the written word. The fragmented nature of trials in Japan (see chapter 6) also works against reliance on oral skills. Nevertheless, the Japanese prosecutor must be able to effectively present the case and to counter defense contentions, should the charges be contested. Even if the defendant admits his guilt in court, evidence must still be presented to the judges for their consideration, both to ensure that the defendant really is guilty and to provide information useful in sentencing.

As might be expected, Japanese prosecutors win most of their cases—a not guilty verdict is rendered in less than 1 percent of all criminal cases heard by district courts (*White Paper on Crime 1988: 17*). Prosecutors also play an important role in sentencing. During the closing argument, the prosecutor makes a sentence recommendation based upon the seriousness of the crime, the character of the defendant, and the demands of society. Although representing the state in an adversary proceeding, the prosecutor in Japan is supposed to be an impartial representative of justice, and therefore the sentence recommendation is usually quite reasonable (Nagashima 1963: 303). Many of the same factors involved in suspension of prosecution decisions are used in sentence recommendations, including the criminological and deterrent considerations discussed above. Although empirical studies of the extent to which Japanese judges follow prosecutorial recommendations are not available, prosecutors think their recommendations are followed quite closely most of the time. Occasionally, as I have noted above, a prosecutor will make a recommendation expecting the judge not to follow it; in these cases it is understood by all concerned that such a recommendation is necessary for political purposes but that the true expectation and desire is something else again.

CONCLUSIONS

Japanese prosecutors clearly play a major role in the criminal justice system. Their clearly constituted authority to indict or to suspend prosecution and to control access of the defendant to his attorney, and their ability to control virtually all aspects of the investigation of the offense, amounts to a quasi-judicial authority, and in fact prosecutors in Japan are considered equal to judges in most respects. Their discretion is rarely challenged and even more rarely curtailed, while their authority is generally accepted by Japanese society. Given their power and authority, abuses are inevitable, but examples of such abuses are not common and the mechanisms that exist for review of prosecutorial decision making as well as the general consensus within Japan on how to deal with crime minimize the potential for abuse of authority. The highly selective criteria used for admission to the Training and Research Institute guarantee a high basic level of competence, while the detailed and extensive policy guidelines regarding prosecution ensure a high level of consistency in decision making. The major role played by prosecutors in recent Japanese political scandals further enhances their reputation as upholders of justice, regardless of the status of the accused.

It should also be noted that an important watchdog function is performed by lawyers and legal organizations who keep a close watch on prosecutorial decision making. The next chapter describes how defense attorneys, while at a distinct disadvantage with respect to prosecutors, nevertheless play an important role in publicizing and criticizing any perceived abuses by prosecutors. Although we are handicapped by a lack of empirical studies of Japanese prosecutorial decision making, the available evidence indicates a balance between societal concerns and criminological concerns with respect to the accused, with perhaps some reluctance to prosecute cases of abuse of authority by public officials. The statistics are impressive; it remains for future scholars to provide details on the manner in which those statistics are generated.

5

Defense

As we have seen, the majority of those who graduate from the Legal Training and Research Institute choose to become lawyers (*bengoshi*). It is doubtful that any of them at the time opt for criminal defense work, and in fact there are very few lawyers in Japan who do exclusively criminal defense work. Those who do very likely are on retainers to *bōryokudan*. There are no professional public defenders in Japan; the indigent are represented by appointed counsel. With the low crime rate and high confession rate there is simply little work in the area of criminal defense. That work that there is, however, is very important, and defense attorneys in Japan play a crucial role in maintaining and advancing the rights of the accused.

The Institute graduate who wishes to practice law must apply to the appropriate bar (one for each district court[44]) for admission, and upon favorable review by the Bar Council the name is forwarded to the Japanese Bar Federation (*Nichibenren*). The lawyer can practice only if his or her name is on the roll of the Bar Federation (Noda 1976: 146). The Japanese lawyer is bound by very much the same rules of ethical conduct as the American lawyer, and is subject to disciplinary sanctions should those rules be violated. Most lawyers in private practice in Japan are solo practitioners engaged in the general practice of law; the massive firms found in major metropolitan areas in the United States are unknown in Japan. Each bar association establishes standard fees for legal work (Koshi 1970: 197-98), and while members of the bar are not required to charge those fees, most

do. There are four categories of fees: initial fee (tesūryō), consultation fee
(kanteiryō), retainer's fee (komonryō) and "thank you" payment (shakin),
or payment for services rendered (ibid.).

Under Article 37 of the Japanese Constitution, anybody accused of a
crime has the right to counsel, and if they cannot afford counsel the
Constitution provides that such counsel be paid for by the government. The
guarantee is implemented through Article 36 of the Code of Criminal
Procedure, which reads:

Where the accused is unable to select a defense counsel for poverty or some other
reasons, the court shall assign defense counsel on behalf of the accused upon his
request. However, this shall not apply where defense counsel has been selected for
him by some person other than the accused.

"Some other reasons" include minority and handicapped status (CCP,
Article 37). Appointed counsel is entitled to travel expenses, per diem, and
housing if necessary in carrying out the defense of the accused. In practice,
defense counsel will submit a bill to the accused upon conclusion of the trail
and the accused will submit, within twenty days of the final judgment of the
court, to the court a request to be excused from payment of the costs of the
defense (CCP, Article 500). Appointment of counsel takes place only after
indictment, even though Article 34 of the Constitution seems to provide for
counsel at an earlier stage of the proceedings: "No person shall be arrested
or detained without being at once informed of the charges against him or
without immediate privilege of counsel." Should an indigent or other
person entitled to appointed counsel need representation prior to
indictment, the Bar Association's Legal Aid Society (Hōritsu Fujo Kyōkai),
the Japanese Civil Liberties Union, and various other sources may provide
such services (Koshi 1970: 65-66). For offenses punishable by less than three
years in prison, the accused who is deemed competent by the court may
represent himself (CCP, Article 289).

One of the chief controversies involving defense counsel in Japan is access
to their clients. As noted in chapter 4, access of defense counsel to the
accused is controlled by the police or the prosecutor (depending on the stage
of the proceedings), under Article 39, Section 3, of the Code of Criminal
Procedure.

The public prosecutor, public prosecutor's assistant officer, and judicial police
official . . . may, when it is necessary for investigation, designate the date, place,
and time of interview and delivery or receipt of [documents or other things] only
prior to the institution of prosecution, provided that such designation does not
unreasonably hold the suspect in check when he exercises his rights for the defense.

The article is ambiguous, and has therefore been the subject of interpretation by appellate courts. In a 1950 case, Baba v. Japan, the Sapporo High

Court found that the prosecutor acted reasonably in allowing defense counsel twenty minutes on the third day of a ten-day detention, and thirty minutes each on the eighth and ninth days. The Supreme Court, in the 1953 decision *Hongo* v. *Japan* (Supreme Court judgment, July 10, 1953), 7 Keishū 1474, found that police restriction of access to a detained suspect of two or three minutes was inadequate (Nagashima 1963: 306). As might be expected, defense attorneys call for greater access while police and prosecutors want to preserve the status quo (ibid.: 306-7). There is no question that limiting access of defense counsel to their clients hinders preparation of a proper defense, and one might ask whether the extraordinarily high confession rate would continue if greater access were granted. Nevertheless, if this were viewed as a serious problem by the public it is likely that the policy would have been changed by now.

Another controversy concerns discovery. Discovery is provided for in Article 299 of the Code of Criminal Procedure:

Before requesting examination of a witness, expert witness, interpreter, or translator, a public prosecutor, the accused, or his defense counsel must give his opponent party, in advance, an opportunity to know the name and address of the person. Where documentary or real evidence is going to be produced for examination, the opponent party must be afforded, in advance, an opportunity to inspect it.

It is clear from the second sentence of the above article that discovery is limited to evidence that is going to be introduced in the trial. Thus, there may be police reports and other evidence that is part of the prosecution's case but that is not going to be introduced at trial that would not be available through discovery (Nagashima 1963: 307). In practice, however, the prosecutor generally makes complete disclosure to the defense except in cases involving white-collar or organized crime, or radical groups (Suzuki 1980: 17-18). It is in these cases where most of the controversy arises, of course. This is a particular problem because defense attorneys almost without exception lack the resources to conduct extensive investigations of their clients' cases, whereas prosecutors have the full resources of the police as well as their own offices. Prosecutors respond that some evidence is very sensitive and can damage the criminal jurstice system if revealed. The debate continues, with judges ruling on a case-by-case basis (see Nagshima 1963: 307-10).

The issue of discovery becomes important in another context as well, and that is the role of defense counsel in consenting to out-of-court statements. Inasmuch as witnesses other than character witnesses are rarely called during a criminal trial in Japan, there is great reliance on affidavits. Because hearsay rules prevent the use of affidavits without consent of the defense (CCP, Articles 320 and 326), there is pressure on the defense to consent to the admission of prosecution evidence. As Goodman points out (1986: 34), the defense has little to gain by objecting unless it thinks it can create substantial doubt with respect to the prosecutor's evidence, since denial of consent will normally result in a defense witness being called, and even if the witness contradicts the prosecutor's evidence there is no guarantee that the court will not admit the evidence anyway. In addition, evidence not admitted for purposes of proof may be used to challenge the credibility of witnesses, including the accused (CCP, Article 328). This makes discovery even more important to the defense, because the defense must prepare a strategy with respect to consent if it is going to be effective, but if it does not have access to the evidence in question until it is offered by the prosecution to the court, such preparation is impossible.

Although the defense attorney is clearly at a disadvantage at the trial stage of the proceedings, he can play an informal role prior to trial. As illustrated in the case study in chapter 2, the defense attorney can play a key role in contacting the victim or victim's family along with the accused in order to make apologies and offer reparations. The lawyer may be able to obtain a written statement of forgiveness (*jidanshō*) and request for leniency from the victim and/or victim's family for submission to the court that, while not mitigating guilt may well mitigate the sentence or play a role in the prosecutor's suspension of prosecution decision. There is nothing to prevent the defense attorney from contacting the prosecutor during the investigative phase of the case to try to persuade the prosecutor not to indict or to recommend a lenient sentence. This does not take place frequently, however; in the average case there is little or no pre-indictment contact between prosecution and defense, and in fact little contact during any phase of the case, unlike the system in the United States where plea bargaining dominates.[45]

As in the United States, the defense may make a number of pretrial motions, including challenging the judge for cause (CCP, Articles 20-26), challenging the jurisdiction of the court or asking for a change of venue (CCP, Article 19), asking for suppression of evidence (CCP, Article 297), or other such motions. These motions are not routinely made, as in the United States, nor need they be made on any special form (Koshi 1970: 80). Japanese courts enforce the exclusionary rule, although the standards for admissibility are not as rigid in Japan as they are in the United States (Tanaka 1984: 822).

The defendant in Japanese trials has the right to silence, but after being warned of that right by the judge the defendant as well as his counsel may make a statement about the charges against him (CCP, Article 311).[46] The judge may question the defendant at any time during the trial about any statements the defendant has made, although this is usually done only after the defense has presented its case (Nagashima 1963: 311). The defendant still retains the right to silence, either by not taking the stand at all or by refusing to answer specific questions on the stand, regardless of whether the

statements may be incriminating or not (CCP, Article 311). The defendant
is not under oath as a witness, and thus cannot be prosecuted for perjury for
any statements made (Nagashima 1963: 312). The defendant can, of course,
be cross-examined by the prosecution. The decision on the part of the
defendant and his counsel on whether or not to take the stand is based, as in
the United States, on a number of factors, not the least of which is the
impression the defendant will make on the court. It is probably safe to say
that, as in the United States, failure to take the stand on the part of the
defendant will be seen in a negative light by the court, although in Japan, of
course, there is no jury. The judge is more likely to be able to subjugate any
prejudices about the lack of testimony by the defendant than is a jury, but
this is balanced by the cultural expectation in Japan that the defendant not
only confess his guilt but show great remorse as well.

The defense attorney in Japan has an important function in presenting to
the court all of the mitigating circumstances in a particular case, regardless
of the plea of the defendant or finding of the court. When the defendant
admits guilt,[47] as most do, the role of the defense attorney becomes one of
persuading the judge to impose a lenient sentence, and the most effective
method of accomplishing this is to effectively present factors in mitigation
of the offense. A primary factor, as discussed above, is restitution and
remorse. The defense attorney does not only present the case to the court
but serves as an advisor to the defendant as well, suggesting to the
defendant how best to make restitution and to show remorse.[48] Other
mitigating factors include attitude, education, work history, family
responsibilities, and lack of criminal record, factors which also play an
important role in suspension of prosecution decisions. If the defendant
does not admit guilt, the role of the defense attorney involves not only
presenting mitigating factors but challenging the evidence presented by the
prosecution. This is rarely successful, given the thoroughness of police and
prosecutorial investigations and reports, but challenging affidavits and
cross-examining witnesses nevertheless is required in any defense, and
frequently works in mitigation of the offense even though failing to
persuade the court of the defendant's innocence.

Some Japanese defense attorneys have called for the reinstatement of the
jury system, arguing that their clients would receive more justice under such
a system than under the present system utilizing professional judges. These
judges, they contend, are much more likely to believe police witnesses and
to accept coerced confessions than would a jury. The Association for Trial
by Jury staged a mock trial in 1988 to test the ability of average Japanese
citizens to render fair and impartial verdicts and concluded that the vast
majority of jurors could return such verdicts. They further argued that the
jury system was more democratic than the system presently used, and that
the jury system had never been given a fair chance to prove itself in Japan.
Whether such criticism will have any effect is difficult to say, but it does

show that the Japanese defense attorneys are not reluctant to challenge the system in order to obtain fair trials for their clients (Gotoh 1989: 20).

While it may sound as if defense attorneys are at a distinct disadvantage in Japan at the pretrial and trial stages of the criminal process, these attorneys have been successful in appeals that have resulted in case law favorable to the accused, as well as having convictions based on coerced confessions overturned (as was discussed in chapter 2). In general, however, appellate court decisions are more likely to support the prosecution than the defense (see Tanaka 1984: 812-32; Itoh and Beer 1978: 154-74). There may be a recent trend in the opposite direction, given the number of reversals of convictions in capital and other serious felony cases in Japan, but it is too early to say for certain whether in fact there is a trend or whether the cases are isolated ones. A 1989 Osaka case illustrates what may be part of a trend toward much closer examination of confessions and physical evidence. A thirty-year-old snack bar owner was arrested in May 1986 for the rape of an eighteen-year-old high school student in Osaka Prefecture, and jailed for fourteen months despite his claims of innocence. He later admitted committing the crime and was indicted by the district prosecutor's office. During the trial, however, he did not admit his guilt and presented an alibi. The prosecution countered with the victim's testimony as well as a sample of the defendant's hair, allegedly found at the scene of the crime. Evidence was presented by the defense pointing out that none of the defendant's fingerprints were found on the beer can allegedly handled by the defendant, that the victim did not seek help when the defendant allowed her to leave the car where the rape allegedly occurred in order to purchase beer, and that the car and a knife allegedly used in the crime were never found. The judge, in finding the defendant not guilty, said that the testimony of the victim was not reliable and that the hair sample was probably fabricated by the prosecution. The defendant's first lawyer, it should be noted, testified for the prosecution that he was convinced of his client's quilt. He later resigned from the case (*The Japan Times* 2/21/89: 2).

The provisions of the Japanese Constitution that protect those accused of criminal acts are very similar to provisions found in the Bill of Rights of the United Stated Constitution, as described in chapter 1. The application and interpretation of these provisions, however, is rather different in the two countries. Article 39 of the Constitution, for example, protects the accused from double jeopardy, but is seemingly inconsistent with the right of the prosecution to appeal not only sentences but not guilty findings of the courts. In *Japan* v. *Ishizaki* (Supreme Court judgment, September 27, 1950), 4 Keishū 1805, the Court found that these powers of the prosecutor do not violate the double jeopardy provisions of the Constitution. And in *Kojima* v. *Japan* (Supreme Court judgment, July 13, 1966), 20 Keishū 6, the Court found that the use by the judge of prior unindicted offenses in determining sentence did not violate the double jeopardy provisions of the

Constitution.[49] In a case involving voluntariness of confessions, *Abe* v. *Japan* (Supreme Court judgment, July 1, 1966), 20 Keishū 537, the Court found that a confession made in return for a promise not to indict could not be used as evidence after an indictment was made, but upheld the conviction nevertheless, finding that other evidence sufficient to convict was present. In a search and seizure case, *Japan* v. *Arima* (Supreme Court judgment, June 7, 1961), 15 Keishū 915, the Court also found for the government. Arima had been named as the source of drugs by a person just arrested for possession of the illegal substance. Officers went to his residence but he was not home. His seventeen-year-old daughter was, however, and gave officers permission to search the house. The search revealed drugs. When Arima arrived home he was confronted with the evidence, whereupon he confessed to possessing and selling drugs. He was found guilty by the district court but appealed. The high court overturned the conviction for possession on the basis that the search and seizure was made before the arrest and without a warrant, that the daughter could not have given informed consent to search since she did not know the implications of her act, and that the search was made on the basis of possession whereas the appellant was arrested for sales. The decision was appealed to the Supreme Court. The Supreme Court reversed the high court, arguing that the Code of Criminal Procedure does not require that arrest always precede search and seizure and that the Constitution allows searches and seizures without a warrant when the arrest takes place closely in time to the search and seizure.[50]

A final example involves Article 205 of the Penal Code, which reads as follows:

1. A person who inflicts a bodily injury upon another and thereby causes his death shall be punished with imprisonment at forced labor for a limited term of not less than two years.
2. When the crime referred to in the preceding paragraph is committed against a lineal ascendant of the offender or of his or her spouse, imprisonment at forced labor for life or for not less than three years shall be imposed.

Although part of the new (post-war) Penal Code, this provision clearly reflects the traditional concept of filial piety. At the same time, it conflicts with equality provisions of the Constitution, particularly Article 14, which states that everyone is equal under the law prohibits discrimination in political, economic, or social relations because of race, creed, sex, social status, or family origin.

This conflict was first addressed in *Japan* v. *Yamato*, the "Fukuoka Patricide Decision" (Supreme Court judgment, October 11, 1950), 4 Keishū 2037, which upheld the constitutionality of Article 205(2). In *Aizawa* v. *Japan* (Supreme Court judgment, April 4, 1973), 27 Keishū 265, however,

Article 200 of the Penal Code, which provides for more severe punishment for murder of a lineal ascendant, was declared unconstitutional as contrary to Article 14 of the Constitution.[51] In *Matsui* v. Japan (Supreme Court judgment, September 26, 1974), 28 Keishū 329, however, the constitutionality of Article 205(2) was again upheld, despite the holding in the *Aizawa* case, on the basis that the difference in the punishments provided for in the two paragraphs is not unreasonably large (Tanaka 1984: 728).

As can be seen, despite the fact that appellate courts in Japan have not been overly supportive of the rights of the accused, defense attorneys have been active in efforts to protect their clients as well as establish principles for future cases. Although there have been few significant rulings on procedural issues in recent years, there have been several important cases overturning convictions in capital cases where confessions have been coerced or were otherwise unreliable (see chapter 2). It would seem, based on the limited information available on criminal defense work in Japan, that the primary role of the defense attorney is in the pre- and post-trial stages of the criminal process, in working for suspension of prosecution or for leniency in sentencing, and in appealing cases where a perceived injustice has taken place. Even though Japan has an adversary system of justice, there is little likelihood that the role of the defense attorney in Japan will ever approximate that in the United States. The Japanese appellate courts have not interpreted the criminal justice provisions of the Japanese Constitution in the same manner that American courts have interpreted essentially the same provisions in the United States Constitution,[52] nor is this likely to change substantially even with a conservative trend in American courts and a liberal trend in Japanese courts. Even more importantly, the history and the culture of the nation to a large extent shape the nature of the adversary process, and this alone will ensure that the role of the defense attorney in Japan remains relatively unchanged for the foreseeable future.

6

The Judiciary

STRUCTURE AND FUNCTION

A structural diagram of the Japanese court system is provided in figure 6.1. As the diagram illustrates, it is a unitary system and is organizationally quite simple. Functionally, it is very similar to court systems found in many states in the United States, with essentially four levels—two trial courts and two appellate courts. Although every prefecture has at least one district court and usually several summary courts, prefectural governments have no control whatsoever over any courts; administrative control comes only from the Supreme Court in Tokyo. There are no municipal or city courts such as in many areas of the United States, and all judicial personnel are employees of the government. Chapter VI of the Japanese Constitution is similar in purpose to Article 3 of the United States Constitution, in that it establishes a Supreme Court and provides for the establishment of inferior courts through legislation (Article 76). It also provides for the administrative powers of the Supreme Court (Article 77), appointment, composition, and removal of judges (Articles 78, 79, and 80), the power of judicial review (Article 81), and for public trials, with certain narrow exceptions (Article 82). The detailed organizational provisions of the judicial system are found in the Court Organization Law (*Saibansho Kōsei Hō*). Both the Constitution and the Court Organization Law (hereafter COL) were, of course, creatures of the occupation and therefore reflect a good deal of

Figure 6.1
Judicial System

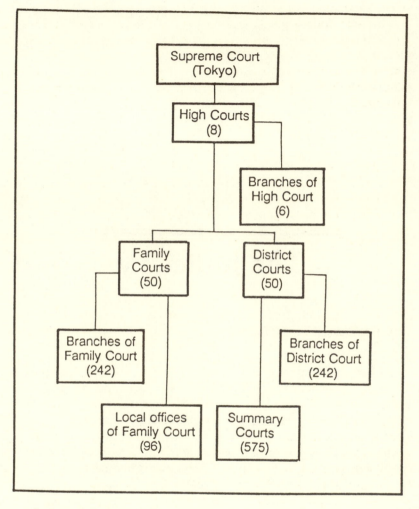

Source: Government of Japan, Ministry of Justice, Supreme Court, "Justice in Japan" (1988), p. 11.

Western thought as well as elements of European and traditional Japanese practice.

As previous chapters indicate, many, if not most, of the criminal cases in Japan are disposed of in the summary courts. There are 575 summary courts in Japan staffed by approximately 790 summary court judges; all cases in summary courts are heard by a single judge. Summary courts have original jurisdiction over minor criminal cases (civil jurisdiction of the various courts is excluded from this discussion), generally those offenses punishable by fines. Summary courts cannot normally impose sentences of imprisonment, although under some circumstances provided for specifically in law they can impose sentences of forced labor for a maximum of three years (*Justice in Japan:* 34). Should a more severe sentence be appropriate, the case must be transferred to the district court. When the summary court is handling a criminal case using summary proceedings (documentry hearing), the maximum punishment is a fine of 200,000 yen. Thus, summary courts may dispose of cases through either a trial or through summary proceedings. A defendant who opts for a summary proceeding does not waive the right to a trial if the outcome of the proceeding is not satisfactory.

The next level of courts is the district and family courts, which, although at the same level, are administratively and jurisdictionally separate. There are 50 family courts (*katei saibansho*), with 242 branches, all located with district courts and their branches. In addition, there are 96 local offices of the family court located with summary courts in the more rural areas of Japan. Approximately 200 judges and 150 assistant judges are assigned to these courts (ibid.: 31). The family court is a court of first instance for all domestic matters, including juvenile delinquency cases (under age twenty) and cases involving injury to, or to the welfare of, juveniles. The 1,500 family court probation officers assigned to family courts play a key role in the operation of these courts, which emphasize rehabilitation (ibid.: 32). Should the rehabilitative approach not be effective or appropriate, the family court may, if the juvenile is over sixteen years of age, refer the case to the prosecutor for disposition in district court as an adult. All family court cases are heard by a single judge and the proceedings are closed to the public.

District courts (*chihō saibansho*) number the same as family courts and are staffed with approximately 900 judges and 460 assistant judges. They are courts of first instance for almost all contested criminal cases, exercising general jurisdiction over all crimes committed in the prefecture within which the court is located.[53] Cases in district court may be heard either by a single judge or by a three-judge panel, or collegiate body. In practice, most cases are heard by a single judge; those heard by the collegiate body include most crimes punishable by death or life imprisonment, those offenses specifically required by law to be heard by a collegiate body, and those cases in which the collegiate body itself decides to exercise jurisdiction (ibid.: 29). Note that there are no preliminary hearings in lower courts and that defendants are not bound over from one court to another as is usually the case in the United States. The only exception to this is the defendant whose case is disposed of through summary procedure but who is dissatisfied with the outcome. Those cases can be heard de novo in district court; the summary procedure is not a preliminary hearing, however, and has no effect on subsequent proceedings.

There are high courts (*kōtō saibansho*) located in eight major cities in Japan: Tokyo, Osaka, Nagoya, Hiroshima, Fukuoka, Sendai, Sapporo, and Takamatsu, with six branch offices of these courts located in other cities. The cities listed above are the largest cities that are centrally located in geographic regions throughout Japan. There are approximately 280 judges assigned to high courts (ibid.: 28). High courts are primarily appellate courts, although they have original jurisdiction in election and insurrection cases; the Tokyo High Court has exclusive and original jurisdiction over appeals from quasi-judicial agencies such as the Fair Trade Commission, Patent Office, and the Marine Accident Inquiry Agency. The high court hears appeals from district, family, and summary courts.[54] Each high court is headed by a president, or senior judge. Cases on appeal are heard by a three-judge panel and original jurisdiction cases are heard by a five-judge court (ibid.). Buildings in which high courts are located also normally contain district, family, and summary courts; buildings in which district courts are located usually house a summary court as well. Thus, in Japan, courts tend to be located in the same buildings, much the way it is in most large cities in the United States, with branches in suburbs and rural areas.

High courts hear *kōso* appeals, the procedure for institution of which is covered in Chapter II of Book III of the Code of Criminal Procedure. *Kōso* appeals may be instituted for a variety of reasons, both substantive and procedural, including jurisdiction (CCP, Article 377), procedural irregularities by the court (CCP, Article 378), misreading of the law CCP, Articles 379 and 380), improper or unjust punishment[55] (CCP, Article 381), or errors in finding facts (CCP, Article 382). The appeal is filed by written motion within fourteen days of the judgment in the original trial court (CCP, Articles 373 and 374), after which a statement of the grounds for the appeal must be filed with the appropriate high court (CCP, Article 376). If the written motion is filed late, the original trial court must dismiss the motion, but immediate *kōkoku* appeal is possible, as described below (CCP, Article 375). There are few limitations on the material the court may examine in such appeals. The court may, for example, examine new material not introduced at the trial or evidence not listed in appellant's brief (CCP, Articles 392 and 393). The high court may reverse the lower court decision and remand for further proceedings or it may pass judgment itself (CCP, Articles 397-400). The high court may also hold a trial under almost all of the provisions of original trials (CCP, Article 404; Dando 1965: 426). Finally, the high court may, with the permission of the Supreme Court, transfer the case to the higher court under certain circumstances (Dando 1965: 433). High courts, then, have substantial discretion and leeway in the manner by which they deal with appeals.

The Supreme Court of Japan (*Saikō Saibansho*) is the court of last resort and exercises administrative control over all courts in Japan. The Court has original jurisdiction only in cases involving impeachment of commissioners of the National Personnel Authority (civil service), and is the highest appellate court for all other cases. The court consists of a chief justice and fourteen justices, and cases may be heard by the entire court (Grand Bench) or by one of three petty benches consisting of five justices each, with quorums of nine and three, respectively, being required (ibid.: 17). All cases are initially assigned to a petty bench, but if the case involves a constitutional issue it is transferred to the Grand Bench. Supreme Court justices are assisted by "research assistants" (chōsakan) who are in fact exceptional judges selected from lower courts. There are thirty research officials assigned to the court. Even though the number assigned works out to two research officials per justice, they are not assigned to individual justices but rather specialize in civil, criminal, or administrative law. Criminal law specialists are assigned to petty benches to assist in criminal appeals (Danelski 1969: 132-33). Technically, the Court must accept all appeals— there being no equivalent to denial of certiorari—but in practice it summarily dismisses approximately 90 percent of the approximately 1,600 criminal cases appealed each year (Itoh 1988: 207). Each petty bench meets twice per week, while the Grand Bench meets only once, on Wednesday (Justice in Japan: 17).

The Supreme Court disposes of approximately 3,400 cases per year. Criminal cases constitute about 45 percent of the total. In 1987, the Court received 1,538 criminal cases, disposed of 1,511, and left 575 pending (ibid.: 21), numbers considerably lower than those in the first two decades of the Court's existence, when the Court disposed of as many as 6,300 cases and left over 4,000 cases pending (Tanaka 1984: 477). The reduction in the number of cases heard has also had the effect of reducing the delays involved in appealing cases, delays that had been highly criticized by Japanese scholars (ibid.: 471, 475-77). In 1986, over 75 percent of all jōkoku appeals were disposed of within two years or less (White Paper on Crime 1988: 103). Delays remain a problem, however, throughout the Japanese judicial system.

There are two types of appeals entertained by the Supreme Court: jōkoku and kōkoku. A jōkoku appeal is an appeal of a judgment in the first or second interest by a high court, a judgment in the first interest by a district, family, or summary court (in the last case when transferred to the Supreme Court by high court as provided for in the Code of Criminal Procedure) (CCP, Article 405), a special appeal against a high court judgment, or an extraordinary appeal by the prosecutor-general (Justice in Japan: 17). Grounds for such appeals in criminal cases are limited to constitutional questions and alleged conflicts with Supreme Court or high court precedent (Itoh 1988: 206). Procedures for initiating jōkoku appeals are virtually the same as for kōso appeals. As in kōso appeals, the Court is not limited by the issues raised by the appellant but can determine whether there are other grounds on which to support an appeal (CCP, Articles 404 and 411). In general, the same provisions that apply to *kōso* appeals apply to *jōkoku* appeals.

The *kōkoku* appeal must be based on alleged constitutional violations or conflict with precedent, as in *jōkoku* appeals, and may be heard by a high court or, in the case of a special *kōkoku* appeal, by the Supreme Court. Article 419 of the Code of Criminal Procedure provides for *kōkoku* appeals against any ruling of a court, except where specifically prohibited. There are two types of general *kōkoku* appeal, ordinary and immediate, both of which would be made to a high court (Dando 1963: 443). *Kōkoku* appeals are used against rulings, as opposed to judgments, of courts and are more informal than *kōso* or *jōkoku* appeals. Immediate appeals must be made within three days of the disputed ruling, they must be made in writing to the original court, and the original court must either make the requested correction or send the appeal to the appropriate high court within three days CCP, (Articles 422 and 423). An immediate appeal has the effect of suspending the execution of the decision of the court, while this may happen at the court's discretion in the case of a regular appeal (CCP, Articles 424 and 425). Regular *kōkoku* appeals cannot be made against a ruling of a high court where an immediate appeal may be made, but there is provision for an "objection" in lieu of such appeal (CCP, Article 428). The "objection" has been called a quasi-*kōkoku* appeal, since it serves the same purpose as a regular *kōkoku* appeal (Dando 1965: 444). This provision allows any party (normally the defendant or accused) to object to decisions relating to bail, detention, fines, articles seized by the police or prosecutors, or restrictions on communications between a suspect and his attorney, among other things (CCP, Articles 429 and 430). Orders not subject to objections can be appealed to the Supreme Court by a special *kōkoku* appeal if the basis of the appeal concerns constitutional issues, conflicting precedent, or against decisions of high courts sitting as courts of *jōkoku* or *kōso* appeal (CCP, Article 433).

JUDGES

Most judges in Japan are graduates of the Legal Training and Research Institute (*Shihō Kenshūsho*). As we have seen in chapter 3, graduates of the Institute may choose to become assistant judges (*hanji-ho*). They must apply for the position to the Supreme Court, which evaluates their qualifications and forwards their nominations to the cabinet, which makes the formal appointment. No nomination has ever been rejected by a cabinet (Tanaka 1984: 555). The term of office of all judges of inferior courts is ten years, with reappointment practically assured. An assistant judge is normally promoted to the status of judge (*hanji*) after ten years. After having served as an assistant judge for three years, however, an assistant judge may be appointed as a judge of a summary court. The assistant judge normally serves as a member of a three-judge panel in district courts until either appointment as a judge or summary court judge. Summary court judges may also be appointed from the ranks of prosecutors or private attorneys with at least three years of experience or from among those with extensive experience in the law and of judicial procedure and who have been recommended by the Summary Court Judges Selection Committee (ibid.: 556). Most of those in this category are former court clerks. Judges of high, district, and family courts must retire at age sixty-five, justices of the Supreme Court and summary court judges at age seventy. Removal of inferior court judges is by impeachment by the Impeachment Court, which is made up of fourteen members of the Diet (*Justice in Japan:* 35).

Those appointed to high, district, or family courts must have been assistant judges, judges of a summary court, prosecutors, private attorneys, instructors at the Judicial Training Institute or Research and Training Institute for Court Clerks, professors or assistant professors at accredited universities or colleges, or officials of the Ministry of Justice, for at least ten years (Koshi 1970: 188). Supreme Court justices are appointed according to a different procedure and criteria. The chief justice is nominated by the cabinet and appointed by the emperor, while the remaining justices are appointed by the cabinet. The emperor's act is symbolic, as no nominations have been rejected. Nominees must be at least forty years of age, and at least ten of the fifteen must have at least ten years experience as presidents of high courts or as judges of high, district, or family courts, or twenty years experience as judges of summary courts, public prosecutors, practicing attorneys, or professors or assistant professors in a recognized law school. The remaining five justices may be selected from among those who are "of broad vision and well grounded in law" (COL, Article 41).

It has been a standard policy to appoint five justices from among career judges, five from practicing attorneys, and the remaining five from among prosecutors, law professors, and civil servants, although the 5-5-5 ratio has not always been followed (Tanaka 1984: 555). Supreme Court justices are subjected to public review at the first general election of members of the House of Representatives following their appointment and again after having served ten years, very much like the process used in the "Missouri Plan" in the United States. None have ever been rejected by the people. Inasmuch as most of the justices are in their early sixties when appointed, and must retire at age seventy, turnover is fairly high (ibid.: 694). Although justices are appointed by the cabinet, the chief justice plays a major role in the selection process, especially if the justice is to be chosen from among career judges (Hattori 1984: 75). Similarly, if the justice is to be chosen from among practicing attorneys, the bar association plays a major role. Although politics does not seem to play much of a role in Supreme Court appointments, certain factors are highly correlated with such appointments. With one exception, all justices selected from among career judges have been presidents of high courts, usually those in either Tokyo or Osaka, and those selected from among practicing attorneys have overwhelmingly been

presidents or vice-presidents of local bar associations in Tokyo and Osaka
(Tanaka 1984: 693). And, of course, a large majority of the justices are
graduates of Tokyo University. This represents not so much an "old boy"
network as a clearly defined career path, although university affiliation
plays the same important role in judicial selection in Japan as it does in the
private sphere.

Judges are assigned to specific courts by the Supreme Court immediately
after their appointment (COL, Article 47), and can expect to serve in that
court for several years before being transferred to another court. Assistant
judges are rotated among a variety of courts of different sizes in different
locations in order to give them as much experience as possible during their
ten-year tenure prior to being promoted to judge. The transfer of a judge
can also be a promotion if that judge is transferred from a small court to a
large court or from a position of lesser responsibility to one of greater
responsibility. Such transfers/promotions may entail an increase in salary
as well (Hattori 1984: 79). Assistant judges almost invariably begin their
careers assigned as a junior member of a three-judge bench in a district
court. Thus, while the newly appointed assistant judge is assigned to a
position where he or she is junior, the new assistant judge will be hearing
the more significant cases, cases that are too complex or important to be
heard by a single judge. After at least five years of conscientious service, the
assistant judge can be designated a specially-qualified assistant judge, which
means that the judge can hear cases alone (ibid.). Further promotions after
being designated a judge would include being assigned as a presiding judge,
as a junior member of a high court bench, or as chief judge of a district or
family court. A few are designated president of a high court or appointed to
the Supreme Court. All promotions and assignments are made by the
Supreme Court, usually in consultation with the judge's immediate
superiors.

TRIAL PROCEDURE

What we in the West think of as a trial bears little resemblance to a trial in
Japan, even though many elements are the same. The primary difference is
that a trial in Japan consists of many separate hearings, each lasting from
less than an hour to one day, with hearings being scheduled every three
weeks or two months. A complex case involving many witnesses and
motions may, therefore, take many months or even years to complete. Such
a case, for example, involving election law violations started formally with
an indictment in May 1983. As of the end of April 1989 there had been over
fifty separate hearings or trial sessions, each lasting from twenty minutes to
three hours in length. Sessions were normally held every month, but on
several occasions there were two- or three-month gaps. At least three judges
and two assistant judges have heard the case, and several prosecutors have
been involved as the case drags on.[56] The case had not been resolved by the
end of 1989. It is not unusual for such political cases to take years to

complete, but even the normal contested criminal case will take several months.

Noncontested criminal cases, which constitute the vast majority of all criminal cases, are usually disposed of with dispatch. In such cases, the judge need only examine written and documentary evidence submitted by the prosecution, although the evidence is subject to challenge by the defense, and in some cases the judge will allow the prosecutor merely to summarize the evidence aloud in open court. In such noncontested cases, rules of evidence (such as the hearsay rule) are relaxed in the interest of efficiency (Araki 1985: 621). The primary role of the judge in these cases is to protect the rights of the accused by examining all of the evidence submitted (and, occasionally, requiring the submission of more evidence) and determining the appropriate sentence. Criminal trials in Japan are not bifurcated, and one of the reasons that there is so much flexibility regarding admissibility of evidence is that the judge makes use of the evidence for sentencing purposes, there being no pre-sentence investigation for adult offenders in Japan.

Cases where there is no confession or where there is a genuine dispute as to the facts of the case are relatively infrequent, but these take up a good deal of time and resources. In such cases, the judge must play the role of impartial adjudicator and fact-finder, a role quite unlike that played most of the time.[57] Trial procedure in contested criminal cases is similar to that in the United States and other Western nations, although the interrupted nature of trials necessarily results in some differences. The first order of business in a trial is identification of the accused, with the judge asking sufficient questions of the accused to be sure that the accused is in fact the person listed on the indictment. The accused is then arraigned—the prosecutor reads the indictment, the judge informs the accused of the right to silence, and the judge asks whether the accused understands the indictment and has anything to say about it. The accused is not asked to plead either guilty or not guilty, but may admit to the allegations in the indictment, in which case the trial normally proceeds in the manner described in the paragraph above. Motions are made after the arraignment, as described in the previous chapter.

As in the United States, the prosecutor makes the opening statement, outlining the facts of the case and how the prosecution intends to prove those facts. This is followed by the opening statement of the defense, which presents its version of the case. These statements are followed by requests for examination of evidence and lists of witnesses by both sides, and might include a request that the court visit the scene of the alleged offense (Koshi 1970: 81-82). The judge (or judges, in a collegiate court) decide the order of witnesses, as there are no distinct prosecution or defense phases of a trial; prosecution witnesses are usually called first, however (ibid.: 82). Witnesses are initially called before the judge as a group, where they are identified, their responsibilities are explained, and they are sworn. Thereafter, only one witness is allowed in the courtroom at a time. Questioning of witnesses is fairly straightforward, with the side calling the witness conducting direct examination and the other side conducting cross-examination. Frequently, however, the judge initiates the questioning of the witness before allowing questioning by either side. The accused also has the opportunity to ask any questions of the witness. Testimony is either recorded on tape or is summarized by the court reporter; there is no method of stenography or shorthand in Japan.

Rules of evidence are similar to those in the United States, with somewhat more flexibility allowed the Japanese judge. Hearsay evidence is not generally admissible, but there are numerous exceptions (see CCP, Article 321), and the general question facing the judge is how useful the evidence will be in determining the facts of the case and how the evidence was obtained, not whether it might prejudice one side or the other. The fact that there is no jury system makes the admissibility of evidence much less of a problem, and few question the ability of the judge to view any evidence with impartiality. As was noted earlier, evidence may be admitted to determine the character of the accused as well as to determine the facts of the case, because the character of the accused plays a much larger role in a Japanese trial than in a similar trial in the United States and many other countries.[58]

Prosecution and defense both present closing arguments, summing up their case. In the case of the prosecutor, the sentence recommendation (*kyūkei*) is made during the closing argument. The defense may focus on mitigating factors during its closing argument. It is not uncommon, in fact, for the defense attorney to admit the guilt of the accused and plead for leniency (Haruo Abe 1963: 330). The accused is also given a chance to make a statement at this point. The judgment is usually handed down within several weeks of the closing arguments. There is no sentencing hearing; the judge simply reviews the record and the notes of the trial in an attempt to reach an appropriate judgment and, if necessary, sentence. Several judgments are possible: conviction (*yūzai*), conviction with suspended sentence (*shikkō yūyo*), not guilty (*muzai*), acquittal (*menso*),[59] and dismissal (*kōso kikyaku*).[60] The last two judgments are technical in nature and involve procedural issues. The judgment is handed down in writing, and includes the facts of the case, the laws involved, the reasoning of the judge, the judgment, and the sentence (Koshi 1970: 86).

Although punishments are specified in the Penal Code for each offense, the judge generally enjoys a great deal of latitude in sentencing. Homicide, for example, is punishable by death or by imprisonment at forced labor for life or for not less than three years (Penal Code, Article 199). Robbery is punishable by imprisonment at forced labor for a limited term of not less than five years;[61] rape by imprisonment at forced labor for a limited term of not less than two years. A "limited term" generally means no more than fifteen years (Penal Code, Article 13) although in aggravated cases the limit is twenty years (Penal Code, Article 14). Judges, then, have a great deal of leeway within the limits prescribed by law and sentences may be reduced by corrections officials. Table 6.1 illustrates judgments and sentences of district

Table 6.1
Number of People Adjudicated by District/Family Courts, by Offense (1986)

Offence	Total (A)	Death	Life	Deter-minate term (B)	Sus-pended execution of sentence (C)	C/B (%)	Suspen-sion with probation	Fine, minor fine	Not guilty (D)	D/A (%)	Others
Total	63,198	5	36	62,328	34,660	55.6	4,618	584	69	0.1	176
Penal Code offences	34,673	5	36	34,365	19,152	55.7	2,293	123	51	0.1	93
Homicide	986	2	8	968	206	21.3	30	—	4	0.4	4
Robbery	690	3	28	655	91	13.9	41	—	1	0.1	3
Bodily injury	3,949	—	—	3,904	1,937	49.6	325	29	6	0.2	10
Extortion	2,718	—	—	2,714	1,401	51.6	245	—	2	0.1	2
Larceny	5,328	—	—	5,322	1,405	26.4	392	—	2	0.0	4
Fraud	4,249	—	—	4,234	1,775	41.9	306	—	6	0.1	9
Rape	703	—	—	702	236	33.6	74	—	1	0.1	—
Arson	409	—	—	408	141	34.6	43	—	1	0.2	—
Gambling	740	—	—	739	602	81.5	30	1	—	—	—
Violent acts	795	—	—	778	220	28.3	36	15	1	0.1	1
Profes-sional negli-gence	10,108	—	—	9,994	8,486	84.9	499	56	15	0.1	43
Others	3,998	—	—	3,947	2,652	67.2	272	22	12	0.3	17
Special Law offences	28,525	—	—	27,963	15,508	55.5	2,325	461	18	0.1	83
Election Law offences	657	—	—	629	621	98.7	—	13	—	—	15
Firearms and swords	810	—	—	807	196	24.3	32	1	1	0.1	1
Stimulant drugs	14,891	—	—	14,867	5,896	39.7	1,371	—	9	0.1	15
Horse Race Law	209	—	—	209	167	79.9	13	—	—	—	—
Road-traffic viola-tions	8,089	—	—	7,996	5,928	74.1	688	54	1	0.0	38
Others	3,869 (439)	—	—	3,455 (252)	2,700 (192)	78.1 (76.2)	221 (24)	393 (185)	7 (2)	0.2 (0.5)	14

Note: Figures in parentheses show the number of adults whose criminal cases under Juvenile Law were adjudicated in family courts.

Source: Annual Report of Judicial Statistics from Government of Japan, Ministry of Justice, Research and Training Institute, "Summary of the White Paper on Crime" (1988), p. 17.

and family courts in 1986. Only .1 percent of all defendants were found not guilty, ranging from a "high" of .4 percent in homicide cases to a low of almost 0 in larceny and road traffic vilations. A majority of those sentenced to a determinate term, however, were given a suspended sentence (*shikkō yūyo*), the large majority of them without concurrent probation.[62] Those eligible for suspended execution of sentence are those who have been sentenced to no more than three years of imprisonment or a fine of 5,000 yen and who have not been sentenced to imprisonment within the previous five years (unless there are extenuating circumstances) (Penal Code, Article 25). Suspensions ranged from highs of 98.7 percent in election law violations, 84.9 percent in professional negligence cases, and 81.5 percent for gambling offenders to lows of 13.9 percent for robbery, 21.3 percent for homicide, and 24.3 percent for firearms and sword violations. Five death sentences were imposed, two for homicide and three for robbery.[63]

One might well conclude, based on the figures in table 6.1, that Japanese judges are rather lenient. The extremely high conviction rate is, of course, a function of the rigorous screening by the prosecutor, which means in effect that there is substantial evidence of guilt in all contested cases ending up in court. Given the fact that the vast majority of those found guilty in court have not been given leniency by the prosecutor in the form of suspended prosecution, it is interesting that so many sentences are suspended by the judge. Japanese legal scholars believe that, for the most part, judges are quite lenient (Haruo Abe 1963: 331-38). Table 6.2 illustrates the relatively light sentences of imprisonment, even for crimes of violence. It should be noted that a large percentage of the offenders so imprisoned are recidivists. See table 6.3 for sentences imposed on mulitple offenders; sentences change little regardless of prior record, except in the category of "one year or less." Table 6.4 indicates that the rate of suspended sentence decreases significantly with frequency of imprisonment, while the rate of revocations of suspension remains relatively steady until the frequency of imprisonment exceeds six. It is also interesting to note that statutory minimum sentences are not always followed by judges; Article 240 of the Penal Code provides for a maximum sentence of death and a minimum of seven years for robbery resulting in death or bodily injury, but table 6.2 shows that in 1986, 174 of a total of 308 offenders sentenced for this offense received sentences of five years or less. Also, crimes against property are often treated with more severity than crimes against the person: 43 percent of those convicted of bodily injury were sentenced to less than one year, while only 27 percent of those convicted of larceny were so sentenced.[64] The following case study of a *yakuza* "hit" provides some insight into the sentencing decision.

Case Study: "Yakuza" Murder

This case begins at approximately 2 P.M. in early February 1988 in a coffee shop located in a medium-sized city in central Japan, where the

Table 6.2
Number of the Convicted Sentenced to Death or Imprisonment by Courts of First Instance, by Offense and Term of Imprisonment (1986)

Offence	Total	Death	Imprisonment with and without forced labour						
			Life	Over 10 years	10 years or less	5 years or less	3 years or less	Less than 1 year	Less than 6 months
Total	74,897	5	36	158	735	2,057	42,559	21,693	7,654
Penal Code offences	46,934	5	36	153	661	1,748	27,772	15,639	920
Homicide	978	2	8	129	340	175	324	—	—
Robbery	686	3	28	13	148	329	164	1	—
Robbery resulting in death, bodily injury	308	3	28	11	92	171	3	—	—
Rape in the course of robbery	40	—	—	2	30	8	—	—	—
Bodily injury	3,904	—	—	—	27	,111	1,881	1,672	213
Bodily injury resulting in death	271	—	—	—	22	90	159	—	—
Extortion	2,714	—	—	—	3	42	2,321	345	3
Larceny	17,224	—	—	—	21	605	11,893	4,648	57
Fraud	4,234	—	—	—	18	148	3,165	876	27
Rape	702	—	—	3	36	161	502	—	—
Arson	408	—	—	6	50	94	258	—	—
Gambling	974	—	—	—	—	—	414	525	35
Violent acts	778	—	—	—	3	14	346	377	38
Professional negligence	9,994	—	—	—	—	1	3,939	5,736	318
Others	4,338	—	—	2	15	68	2,565	1,459	229
Special Law offences	27,963	—	—	5	74	309	14,787	6,054	6,734
Election Law	629	—	—	—	—	—	269	333	27
Firearms and swords	807	—	—	1	10	69	612	85	30
Stimulant drugs	14,867	—	—	4	61	219	12,081	2,490	12
Horse Race Law	209	—	—	—	—	—	126	79	4
Road-traffic violations	7,996	—	—	—	—	—	54	1,732	6,210
Others	3,455	—	—	—	3	21	1,645	1,335	451

Source: Annual Report of Judicial Statistics from Government of Japan, Ministry of Justice, Research and Training Institute, "Summary of the White Paper on Crime" (1988), p. 99.

number-two man in a local *bōryokudan* was having coffee with some friends. After leisurely drinking his coffee and chatting, he and an associate started across the street. As he stepped off the curb, a car pulled in front of the *yakuza* boss and its two occupants opened fire. The victim turned to run back toward the coffee shop and was hit once in the back, staggering into the coffee shop parking lot and collapsing. Neither his associate nor a cab driver who had followed them out of the coffee shop was hit. The victim's friends rushed him to a nearby hospital, where he died at about 4:30 P.M. from massive damage to internal organs. The victim was thirty-nine, married, and the father of one child.

Table 6.3

Ratio of Types of Punishment and Term of Imprisonment for Subjects with Multiple Previous Convictions, from First to Tenth Convictions

Frequency of conviction	Imprisonment with or without forced labour											over 3 years	Fine	Penal detention Minor fine others
	3 months or less		6 months or less		1 year or less		2 years or less		3 years or less				
		As to suspended execution of sentence		As to suspended execution of sentence		As to suspended execution of sentence		As to suspended execution of sentence		As to suspended execution of sentence			
1 time	0.8	(0.6)	5.0	(3.4)	30.5	(20.9)	11.5	(4.3)	3.6	(0.7)	2.0	41.8	4.9
2	1.5	(0.5)	7.4	(2.7)	25.6	(9.3)	11.0	(1.4)	2.3	(0.2)	1.2	45.8	5.2
3	2.2	(0.6)	8.2	(2.4)	22.6	(5.5)	12.4	(0.9)	2.1	(0.1)	1.1	46.3	5.1
4	2.2	(0.6)	8.5	(2.1)	20.4	(4.1)	13.5	(0.8)	2.3	(0.1)	1.1	47.1	4.8
5	2.2	(0.6)	8.6	(2.0)	19.1	(3.6)	13.9	(0.7)	2.9	(0.1)	1.3	47.6	4.5
6	2.2	(0.5)	8.7	(2.1)	18.5	(3.0)	13.9	(0.6)	3.4	(0.1)	1.5	47.6	4.2
7	2.2	(0.5)	9.0	(2.1)	18.4	(3.0)	13.7	(0.8)	4.0	(0.1)	1.9	46.7	4.0
8	2.1	(0.5)	9.2	(2.3)	18.3	(2.9)	13.9	(0.8)	4.3	(0.1)	2.1	46.6	3.6
9	2.2	(0.5)	9.1	(2.3)	18.2	(3.3)	14.4	(0.9)	4.7	(0.1)	2.7	45.4	3.4
10	1.9	(0.4)	8.7	(2.3)	17.9	(3.5)	14.7	(1.0)	5.6	(0.1)	3.2	44.9	3.1

Notes: 1. Each figure in the table shows the ratio against the total number of 45,755 multiple convictions counted as 100.0.

2. Figures in parentheses show the ratio of offenders granted a suspension of execution of their sentence.

Source: Government of Japan, Ministry of Justice, Research and Training Institute, "Summary of the White Paper on Crime" (1988), p. 30.

The victim's associate, the cab driver, and three people in the coffee shop witnessed the shooting, but no license number of the suspect vehicle was obtained, nor was there even agreement on the number of occupants in the vehicle. There was general agreement, supported by forensic evidence, that the shots were fired from a distance of six to fifteen feet. Police strongly suspected that the murder was committed by members of a rival gang, but they had no specific suspects. There was known to be conflict between the two gangs, however, so the investigation focused on that theory.

Two week after the shooting, two people showed up at the police station, turned in two .38 caliber handguns, and stated that they had committed the murder. The suspects, ages twenty-two and thirty, were known members of the rival gang and told the police that they had been ordered to kill the boss of the gang but had mistaken the second-in-command for the boss. They had been paid 2,000,000 yen for the killing but had spent most of it by the time they turned themselves in. They refused to say who had ordered them to do the shooting and said they were willing to go to prison for the crime. Despite the fact that the case seemed a simple one, the police and

Table 6.4

Revocation Rate of Suspended Execution of Sentence for Multiple Convicted Prisoners by Frequency of Imprisonment

Frequency of imprisonment	Rate of non-suspended execution of sentence	Rate of suspended execution of sentence	As to suspended execution of sentence with probation	Rate of revocations	As to suspended execution of sentence with probation
1 time	43.6	56.4	11.8	62.9	78.6
2	81.6	18.4	10.0	67.8	76.8
3	93.1	6.9	3.4	61.6	70.7
4	95.2	4.8	1.8	58.5	66.6
5	95.2	4.8	1.7	57.5	68.3
6 or more	95.0	5.0	1.5	39.7	51.2

Notes: 1. Each figure in the table shows the ratio against the total number of 21,885 multiple imprisonments counted as 100.0.
2. Rate of revocation

$$= \frac{\text{revocation of suspended execution of sentence}}{\text{revocation} + \text{non-revocation of suspended execution of sentence}} \times 100$$

3. As to suspended execution of sentence with probation among the rate of revocation as follows:

Rate of revocation of suspended execution of sentence

$$= \frac{\text{revocation of suspended execution of sentence with probation}}{\text{revocation} + \text{non-revocation of suspended execution of sentence with probation}} \times 100$$

Source: Government of Japan, Ministry of Justice, Research and Training Institute, "Summary of the White Paper on Crime" (1988), p. 31.

prosecutors conducted an extensive investigation, in part to be certain that the two suspects actually committed the offense and were not taking the rap for their superiors and in part to add to their knowledge about *bōryokudan* activities. The suspects cooperated with the police in reconstructing the crime, demonstrating how they had sat in their car waiting for the victim to leave the coffee shop, how they did the actual shooting, and where they dumped the shell casings. The suspects told police that they had fired a total of ten shots, using one Smith & Wesson five-shot, two-inch revolver, and one Smith & Wesson six-shot, two-inch revolver.[65] Police could only account for four bullets: one in the victim, one in a nearby car fender, one in a tire, and one in a metal pole in the parking lot. The others must have been fired high, passing over the coffee shop. Police reports included numerous photographs of the bullet holes, the victim, the general scene, and the reenactment, as well as multiple diagrams and statements of witnesses.

Both suspects were indicted. Although their cooperation with the police (except for naming the person who ordered the killing) might be seen as a mitigating factor, in reality hitmen are usually ordered by their bosses to surrender, as this not only reduces police pressure on the gang but also reduces the threat of retaliation by the rival gang. Assailants in such cases are not only paid well for such a crime but their families are taken care of by the gang while the killers are in prison. The fact that the shooting was so public, that it involved firearms, that so many shots were fired, and that the victim in no way provoked the crime made the crime an aggravated one, and prosecutors were determined to ask for lengthy imprisonment. After discussion between the investigating prosecutor, trial prosecutor, and their supervisor, it was determined that the sentence recommendation would be eighteen years for the older defendant and sixteen years for the younger. The killers were sentenced in mid-August 1988 to seventeen and fifteen years, one year less than the recommendations in each case.

Were the sentences lenient? This is a subjective question, but they are probably lighter sentences than would have been imposed in a United States courtroom, where the defendants would have been considered hired killers. A more appropriate question, however, is whether they were lenient within the Japanese context, and to that I think the answer must be no. The sentences were one year less than recommended by the prosecutor, very likely because the judges wanted to show some judicial independence, and the prosecutors' recommendations were significantly greater than the average sentence. As table 6.2 illustrates, sentences of over ten years for homicide are clearly in the minority, but of course the circumstances of homicides differ widely. There were more aggravating factors in this case than there were mitigating factors, and the sentences reflect that fact. It is difficult to make a judgment with respect to leniency on the part of Japanese judges by merely looking at statistics. Each case is different, and the judge has far more information about the case than the average citizen as well as far more experience in the criminal justice system, thereby placing him in a unique position with respect to sentencing. We cannot, therefore, conclude that Japanese judges are either more or less lenient than their counterparts in other countries.

APPELLATE DECISION MAKING

Many important decisions are made by high courts, just as a large number of significant decisions are made by circuit courts of appeal in the United States, but ultimately it is the Supreme Court that has the largest impact on the law of a nation. We will, therefore, focus on the Supreme Court of Japan in this section.[66]

As has been noted previously, the Supreme Court plays a major role in administering the Japanese judiciary, ranging from operation of the Legal Training and Research Institute to the assignment of judges. It is also responsible for in-service training of judges, which includes various programs for assistant judges as well as exchange programs and seminars for more senior judges (Hattori 1984: 80-82), and is responsible for general administrative supervision of judges. Under Article 77 of the Constitution, the Supreme Court has the power of rule-making "under which it determines the rules of procedure and of practice, and of matters relating to attorneys, the internal discipline of the courts and the administration of judicial affairs." The Supreme Court has promulgated over 150 rules, approximately one-third of which relate to procedure (ibid.: 84). In a unitary judicial system such as Japan's, the administrative role of the Supreme Court is a substantial one and has a profound effect on all judicial matters in the country.

Important as its administrative role is, it is the power of judicial review of the Court that is the most noteworthy. Unlike the United States Supreme Court, the power of judicial review of the Japanese Supreme Court is relatively new. Such a power was unknown under the Meiji Constitution. It was provided for initially under the 1947 Constitution, which was modeled in part on the United States Constitution.[67] Just how it was to be exercised was decided in *Suzuki* v. *Japan* (Supreme Court judgment, October 8, 1952), 6 Minshū 801, which resulted from a challenge of the constitutionally of the newly established National Police Reserve and a not-so-subtle attack by an opposition party on the power of the cabinet (Bolz 1980: 98-100). In *Suzuki* the court clearly rejected the role of special constitutional court, finding that Article 81 of the Constitution did not require the Court to assume such status and that the Court would consider constitutional questions only within the framework of true cases and controversies.

The Court initially assigns all cases to one of the three petty benches, where the research clerks (*chōsakan*) review the case and report the results of their analysis to the bench. The review initially is to determine the importance of the case. Inasmuch as the vast majority of criminal appeals are not worthy of review, only a few are researched extensively by the clerk, the rest being stamped with an "X" to indicate a recommendation of dismissal (Danelski 1969: 133). Those deserving of review and researched by the clerk are presented to the bench in the form of a printed report, which is often quite large. The justice to which the case was assigned sets a date for discussion, which he subsequently leads. Rules of discussion and voting are informal. If the bench votes to dismiss, that is the end of the case. If there is the possibility of reversal, appellee will be notified to file a brief and a date for oral argument will be set (ibid.: 134). Oral argument is quite formal, often taking more than one hour, with relatively little questioning by the justices. After oral argument a date is again set for discussion, at which time the case is usually decided. The opinion is written by the justice to whom the case was assigned, unless he is in the minority. Most decisions are unanimous and dissents are rare.

Should the case involve a constitutional question with no precedent or a very complicated or politically significant issue, the case will be referred from a petty bench to the Grand Bench. The decisional process of the Grand Bench is very like that of the petty benches, but due to the nature of the cases before them, the discussions usually last longer and are more spirited (ibid.: 135). For reasons related primarily to culture, discussions of cases among justices of the Japanese Supreme Court are not likely to become as heated or personal as has often been the case on the United States Supreme Court. The need for consensus, conciliation, and unanimity shapes the nature of discussion on the Court; and while justices not only have the right to dissent but are expected to do so should they feel strongly enough about the matter, dissent, at least in recent years, is not common. Concurring opinions, on the other hand, are quite common, often reflecting differences of opinion that in another culture would have been expressed in the form of a dissent.

An important connstitutional case, such as *Japan* v. *Arima* (cited in the previous chapter), illustrates the various types of opinions discussed above. As we have seen, the Supreme Court upheld the police search and seizure, overturning the decision of the Osaka High Court. The majority opinion was that of nine of the justices. The majority opinion first dismissed the contention that the lower court had erroneously applied precedent and then proceeded to discuss the fundamental question raised by the case: whether Article 220 of the Code of Criminal Procedure is consistent with Article 35 of the Constitution, and if so, whether the police officers in this case acted accordingly. Article 35 of the Constitution reads (in part):

The right of all persons to be secure in their homes, papers, and effects against entries, searches, and seizures shall not be impaired except upon warrant issued for adequate cause and particularly describing the place to be searched and things to be seized, or except as provided in Article 33 [which requires a warrant for arrest except when the offense is observed by an officer].

Article 220 of the CCP reads (in part):

When a [police officer] arrests a suspect [pursuant to a warrant] or he arrests a flagrant offender [at the scene of a crime], he may, if necessary, take the following measures. . . :
 (1) To enter the dwelling of a person, or any premises, buildings, or vessels guarded by that person, and search for the suspect;
 (2) To seize, search, or inspect at the place of arrest.

The majority found that Article 35 of the Constitution should be construed to constitute an exception to the principle of requiring a warrant for searches and seizures if the search and seizure are reasonably conducted incident to an arrest, and therefore Article 220 of the CCP, which allows search and seizure without a warrant incident to arrest, is constitutional.

Further, a prior decision found that Article 210 of the CCP, which authorizes arrest without a warrant under urgent conditions, was consistent with the Constitution, and that while there must be a close temporal relationship between arrest on the one hand and search and seizure on the other, which comes first is not relevant. The Court found that the arrest was under conditions of urgency and that the search and seizure was in such close temporal proximity to the arrest that it should be considered incidental to the arrest and therefore constitutional. Inasmuch as the lower court found that search and seizure must follow an arrest and that it was therefore unconstitutional, the lower case judgment must be quashed. Three justices concurred with the result in the case, but felt that the evidence was admissible simply because it was not objected to by the defense. The concurring opinion, therefore, avoided the constitutional issue. The two dissenting justices thought, like the lower court, that both Article 220 of the CCP and Article 35 of the Constitution should be interpreted literally, which would require search and seizure to follow arrest. That there was a dissent at all was an indication of substantial differences of opinion, even though the dissent was not strongly worded. The concurring justices seemed to be of the opinion that the Court should have exercised judicial self-restraint and not reached the constitutional issue.[68]

One of the reasons that there are frequently concurring opinions in Supreme Court cases is that Article 11 of the Court Organization Law states that "the opinion of every judge shall be expressed in written decisions." While it may seem that such a requirement would result in overly long (and confusing) opinions, it was probably intended to clearly change the previous policy that prohibited dissenting opinions (Bolz 1980: 132). The rule is not followed in every case, but it probably does have the effect of encouraging concurring opinions. Because Japan is a civil law nation, one might assume that concurring opinions would have little, if any, effect on the law, but just the opposite is true; concurring opinions carry much more weight relative to majority opinions than is the case in the United States. The overall weight of a Supreme Court judgment, however, is clearly less than it would be in the United States.

A quorum for the Supreme Court consists of eleven justices, and it takes agreement among eight of the justices to find a statute unconstitutional (Supreme Court Rules, Articles 7 and 11). The Court generally exercises judicial self-restraint, however, rarely invalidating either a law or an administrative action, and while the Court usually holds a trial de novo in reviewing challenges to administrative action, it normally upholds the exercise of administrative discretion (Itoh 1988: 210). As chapter 5 explained, the Court tends to take a conservative position in criminal cases, in general upholding trial court judgments as well as legislative enactments and rules of procedure. Some Japanese scholars have attributed this conservative tendency to the fact that all Supreme Court justices to date were socialized during the Meiji era as well as to the effect of Confucianism and Shintoism on the Japanese legal culture (Itoh 1988: 210-11). As Itoh puts it:

The stress for harmony has led to groupism in which collective interests supercede individual interests. Decisions are always group products, and a vote is seldom taken either in the cabinet or in the Supreme Court. The Supreme Court is the only tribunal in which dissents are published, but only the majority opinion is made known in lower courts.

Although there is little question that Itoh's analysis is correct, one should not be left with the impression that there is a great deal of consensus on the Court.

That there are dissents taking place inside a legal culture that places such a premium on harmony and conformity, and that there are concurring opinions that differ substantially from the majority opinion, indicates that there are clear differences of opinion on the Court. Just what accounts for these differences of opinion is more difficult to determine. An early study of the Court using the then-sophisticated techniques of linkage analysis, smallest space analysis, and various statistical measures of correlation, found rather clearly defined voting patterns, groups of justices identifiable by ideology, and a general trend toward sympathy for the criminal defendant (Danelski 1969: 137-50).[69] David Danelski found justices divided into what he called liberal, moderate, and conservative voting blocs and was able to identify one clearly-defined dimension of voting in the area of fair procedure, a component of liberalism (ibid.: 144-45). He also found differences in voting on the three petty benches, with the first bench dominated by conservatives and moderates and the second by liberals, with the third bench more evenly divided between the three ideologies (ibid.: 147-48). He further found that justices who had previously been lawyers were more liberal than those from other backgrounds (judges, bureaucrats, etc.), as were graduates of nonimperial universities as compared to graduates of Tokyo and Kyoto Universities (ibid.: 148).

Danelski's findings seem to contradict our analysis of Supreme Court decisions in criminal procedure cases, but the seeming contradiction can probably be explained in terms of when the analyses were done as well as by the methodology used. And while he identifies a liberal tendency toward criminal defendants, he also found a general conservative trend on the Court. It must be remembered that the Liberal Democratic Party has dominated Japanese politics since World War II and that therefore the justices appointed to the Supreme Court reflect the generally conservative nature of this party.[70] A study by James Dator (1967) done during the same period as Danelski's illustrated the basically conservative nature of Japanese high court judges. Characterizing those judges as "moderately conservative," Dator concluded that their outlook was modern but their ideology was conservative, very much like the general population (Dator 1967: 438).[71] Recent victories of oppositions parties, especially the Socialist Party of Japan, may result in significant changes in appointments, perhaps in the relatively near future, given the high rate of turnover on the Court, with a concomitant liberalizing trend in decisions. Danelski, however, made the same prediction in the last paragraph of his article, which was written in 1966. Nevertheless, justices who were socialized after the war are being appointed to appellate courts, and while they reflect the conservative politics of the LDP, they are not averse to ruling against the party, nor are they as influenced by the Meiji era legal system as were their predecessors.

CONCLUSION

The basic function of courts at all levels in Japan is essentially the same as it is in Western nations, but the manner in which they carry out those functions tends to be dissimilar. Trials are discontinuous and not bifurcated, noncontested cases must still be heard by a judge (unless summary proceedings are used), the order of appearance of witnesses is determined by the judge, and the vast majority of contested cases result in findings of guilty. Almost all judges receive the same training, including a ten-year apprenticeship, and important cases at the trial level are heard by a collegiate court. All judges except those on the Supreme Court are appointed by the Supreme Court, while Supreme Court justices are appointed by the cabinet according to a ratio intended to provide diversity on the Court. There is a good deal of consensus on the Supreme Court and a general trend toward the conservative in criminal matters, but the Court does serve as a guardian of civil liberties as well as a reflection of the ideals of the general population.

As in other aspects of the Japanese criminal justice system, it is difficult, if not methodologically suspect, to compare Japanese courts with those in other countries in qualitative terms, and therefore such comparison will not take place here. It is sufficient to say that the essential judicial functions are carried out in Japan, that the criminal law and rules of criminal procedure are followed very closely, and that judges, while somewhat more restricted in some aspects of the criminal process than those in the United States, nevertheless exercise a good deal of discretion. It is also safe to say that Japanese judges are well trained and respected. To what extent they are responsible for the lauded crime statistics in Japan remains to be discussed in the last chapter, but it can be said at this point that they clearly play a major role in the efficient operation of the Japanese criminal justice system.

7

Corrections

The prosecutor in Japan, as explained in chapter 5, plays an important role in the corrections process, primarily through suspension of prosecution, a process whereby the prosecutor determines that prosecution is not warranted for social or criminological reasons. This prevents the presumably guilty person from having the stigma of a conviction and facilitates his or her integration into law-abiding society, an important stage in the rehabilitation of the offender. The prosecutor also plays an important role in sentencing, because prosecutor's recommendation is weighed heavily by the judge (and the prosecutor can appeal a sentence he thinks is too light). Finally, enforcement of the sentence is the responsibility of the prosecutor (CCP, Article 472). If the offender is convicted of more than one offense and there is more than one penalty, normally the more severe penalty is carried out first, but the prosecutor has the discretion to stay the execution of the more severe penalty while the lesser penalty is executed (CCP, Article 474). The prosecutor does not, of course, have responsibility for the physical custody of the offender or for supervising probation or parole during the offender's sentence, because the prosecutor turns over the offender to the appropriate correctional authorities who, like the prosecutor, are employed by the Ministry of Justice.

Should the offender receive a sentence of probation, almost always in conjunction with a suspended execution of sentence,[72] the responsibility for supervising the probationer falls to a Probation Office[73] (*Hogo Kansatsujo*), an agency under the Rehabilitation Bureau of the Ministry of Justice. There is an office associated with each district/family court. In 1987, this office received 6,477 offenders whose sentences were suspended and who were placed on probation, over half of whom had terms of probation not exceeding three years (*White Paper on Crime 1988:* 19). Almost 70 percent of those on probation successfully completed their terms of probation (ibid.). Probation in Japan is essentially the same as probation in the United States, with probation officers supervising probationers and assisting them in obtaining and keeping jobs, checking on their progress, enforcing the terms of probation as imposed by the court, and, where necessary, revoking probation. As may be seen in table 6.1, even those found guilty of robbery and homicide can be given suspended sentences with probation. As in the United States, probation officers have heavy caseloads, usually numbering over 100 probationers, and therefore they are frequently assisted by volunteer probation officers (Ochiai 1984: 408). Volunteer probation officers are citizens who volunteer for the position, meet certain minimum qualifications,[74] and who are then appointed by the Ministry of Justice for a two-year term, with possibility of reappointment (ibid.). These volunteers are paid only expenses such as travel—they receive no salary for their work.

Incarceration is the responsibility of the Correction Bureau of the Ministry of Justice, which has eight regional offices, located in conjunction with high courts and high prosecutors' offices. The Correction Bureau administers: 58 adult prisons, including 4 for women, 3 medical prisons, 2 for traffic offenders, 1 for United States military prisoners convicted by Japanese courts, and 9 branch prisons; 7 detention houses with 106 branches; 9 juvenile prisons; 59 juvenile training schools; 51 juvenile classification homes with 1 branch; and 3 women's guidance homes (Johnson and Hasegawa 1987: 66). There are, in addition to the facilities listed above, over 1,000 jails administered by the National Police Agency used primarily as temporary detention facilities but which can be used as regular prisons or detention facilities when needed (Nomura 1987: 7). In addition to Yokosuka Prison for United States military prisoners, Fuchū Prison in Tokyo accommodates foreign male prisoners, while Tochigi Prison, in Tochigi Prefecture, accommodates foreign female prisoners (Johnson and Hasegawa 1987: 69). Correctional facilities are located throughout Japan, with more populous regions having more than those with less population.

A major function of the Japanese correctional process is initial classification of offenders, a classification that is designed to determine the appropriate facility for the specific offender as well as the appropriate program within that facility. One adult institution in each of the eight regions serves as a classification center, to which those under twenty-six years of age with sentences of one year or longer who have never been incarcerated are sent for initial classification. The normal period of classification is about two months, during which time the offenders are oriented to prison life, tested for vocational aptitude, counseled, and assigned to appropriate institutions and programs. Additional classification lasting about one week takes place at the assigned institution (*Criminal Justice in Japan* 1983: 29-30). Those not initially assigned to a classification center are evaluated at the place of confinement when their sentences become final and at the prisons to which they are ultimately assigned (ibid.). Classification of juveniles takes place at juvenile classification homes, located in areas where family courts are established. The Juvenile Law specifies a stay of fourteen days in juvenile classification homes, a stay that may be extended for another fourteen days by the court. Juveniles and adults are interviewed and tested in order to determine their appropriate classification.[75] Classification categories are as follows (ibid.: 30-32):

Custodial Considerations

Class A: less advanced criminal inclinations

Class B: more advanced criminal inclinations

Class F: foreigners

Class I: those sentenced to imprisonment without labor

Class J: juveniles

Class L: those sentenced to terms of eight years or more

Class M: mentally defective (includes three sub-categories)

Class P: those in ill health, handicapped, or senile

Class W: females

Class Y: adults under twenty-six years of age

Treatment Considerations

Class E: need for schooling

Class G: need for guidance in daily life (primarily juveniles)

Class O: suitable for open treatment

Class N: suitable for accounting work

Class S: need for special protection and care

Class T: need for therapeutic treatment

Class V: need for vocational training

This rather detailed classification system attempts to best match the offender with an institution and program, and given the large number of institutions and possible programs one would expect it to be quite successful. Some of the institutions have open labor camps attached to them, to which those whose terms are near their end as well as specially selected other prisoners are assigned (ibid.: 32-33).

Those sentenced to imprisonment with labor are expected to work. When appropriate, such labor is combined with vocational training, with the purpose of learning good work habits, learning new skills, and receiving income for work produced. Prison labor used to be almost exclusively agricultural in nature, but has since expanded to include furniture construction, printing, automobile repair, clothing manufacture, and barbering, among other skills (Johnson and Hasegawa 1987: 66; *Criminal Justice in Japan* 1983: 33). The normal work week is forty-four hours long, as in Japan in general. Seven institutions have special intensive vocational training programs, the successful completion of which results in the attainment of a professional certificate from the Ministry of Labor (Nomura 1987: 8). Japanese corrections officials see a strong relationship between lack of occupational skills and/or suitable work habits and crime, and therefore place a good deal of effort in developing these characteristics among the prison population.

Education is available to both adult and juvenile offenders, including programs leading to diplomas. One juvenile facility, the Matsumoto Juvenile Prison in Nagano Prefecture, includes a branch of the local junior high school (*Criminal Justice in Japan* 1983: 33), while other facilities offer junior and senior high school courses. There are also opportunities to take correspondence courses in academic or vocational subjects that, upon successful completion, may provide credits at the junior or senior high or university level. There are no college courses as such offered in Japanese prisons. All educational programs and courses in correctional facilities must be approved by the Ministry of Education. In juvenile institutions, those who have not completed the compulsory nine years of education are required to take basic academic courses, while older students who have completed the required nine years are offered more advanced academic and/or vocational courses. Short-term juvenile offenders, usually sentenced for driving offenses resulting in injury or death, receive an intensive program designed for the specific offense; in the case of the negligent driver, for example, the program emphasizes safe driving and respect for human life (Nomura 1987: 9). Tables 7.1 and 7.2 illustrate the number of graduates of various vocational training courses and skills licenses granted.

Juveniles receive, in addition to the academic and vocational education cited above, guidance in daily living, which deals with such basic subjects as health, hygiene, and responsibility. This program progresses from entry level directed learning to advanced nondirected group discussions and club activities. Volunteer counselors, including individuals representing various religious groups, play an important role in the guidance program, offering moral as well as practical advice to the juvenille offenders (*Criminal Justice in Japan* 1983: 38). These volunteers serve, like the volunteer probation officers, without pay, receiving compensation for expenses only. There were over 1,100 such visitors who made over 11,600 visits in 1987 (*White Paper on Crime 1988:* 116). Given the rather rigid structure and behavioral norms of Japanese life, there is considerable difficulty in reaching those juveniles who have not previously been socialized in those norms, and there are some who simply cannot or will not be reached. Nevertheless, the

Table 7.1
Number of Graduates of Each Vocational Training Course (fiscal year 1987)

Courses	Number of graduates	Courses	Number of graduates
Total	1,580	Horticulture	18
Machinery operation	41	Barbering	57
Sheet-metal processing	22	Laundry	49
Welding	341	Japanese Typewriting	16
Electric wiring	100	Seamanship	8
Western-style tailoring	9	Auto driving	64
Auto repair	80	Farming	3
Carpentry	85	Ceramics	4
Plumbing	17	Making scrolls, etc.	24
Plastering	123	Heavy-goods conveyance (Tama kake)	18
Woodcraft	58		
Printing	41	Leathercraft	5
Mimeographing	17	Gardening	14
Tatami-mat making	51	Computer programming	16
Woodcarving	12	Sewing	49
Boiler operation	80	Knitting	5
Operation of construction machinery	73	Hair-styling	14
		Housekeeping	16
Radio operation	19	Shoemaking	1
Painting	26	Papermaking	1

Source: Correction Bureau, Ministry of Justice from Government of Japan, Ministry of Justice, Research and Training Institute, "Summary of the White Paper on Crime" (1988), p. 117.

attitude toward juvenile offenders in Japan tends to be one of optimism with emphasis on rehabilitation in an attempt to divert the juvenile from a life of crime before the opportunity is no longer available.[76]

Japanese prisons, unlike those in many other nations, are not overcrowded, although there are many facilities that are in need of repair (Johnson and Hasegawa 1987: 67). The trend in prison admissions has been decreasing or levelling in recent years: from a high of 70,727 in 1948, admissions decreased to a low of 25,728 in 1973 and have increased slightly to 29,726 in 1987. Given the increase in the population during this period of time, there has been virtually no increase in terms of prisoners as a percentage of population. Violence in prisons is quite low, as are escapes. In 1987, there were only three escapes, four homicides or serious injuries of prisoners, and eight suicides. There were no attacks on correctional officers or accidental deaths of prisoners (*White Paper on Crime 1988:* 116). With an average daily prison population of over 55,000, these figures are remarkable, especially given the fact that the vast majority of offenders are in Class B, having "advanced criminal tendencies" (ibid.: 115). It would

Table 7.2
Results of Examinations to Obtain Skills Licenses (fiscal year 1987)

Item	Number of examinees	Successful examinees
Total	3,012	2,393
Welder	379	316
High-voltage electrical engineer	8	7
Electric-wiring engineer	88	69
Auto repairer	126	116
Boiler operator	119	84
Barber	55	55
Hairdresser	16	16
Laundry worker	42	39
Auto driver	97	92
Cook	24	17
Dangerous materials' operator	399	313
Skills training courses	714	704
Others	945	565

Source: Correction Bureau, Ministry of Justice from Government of Japan, Ministry of Justice,
Research and Training Institute, "Summary of the White Paper on Crime" (1988),
p. 118.

seem that despite the fact that prisoners in Japan have seriously violated the norms of their society, they still abide by at least some of those norms even while incarcerated.

CORRECTIONS PERSONNEL

The Corrections Bureau of the Ministry of Justice is responsible for the recruitment and training of all correctional officers. All prospective officers must pass an examination to be admitted to the Training Institute for Correctional Personnel in Tokyo or one of its eight branches and must successfully pass the 220-day training course to be appointed as correctional officers (Johnson and Hasegawa 1987: 68). Although the minimum educational requirement for a correctional officer is graduation from high school, many officers, especially those who are female, have two- or four-year college degrees. Younger corrections officers are increasingly being appointed, widening the gap between the ages of the staff and the prisoners: in 1985, 46 percent of the prison staff was under thirty years of age while only 10 percent of the prisoners were in that category, the largest percentage (37 percent) being in the thirty-one to forty age bracket (ibid.: 69). While such disparities might be of little significance in the United States, it does cause problems in Japan, where seniority is the primary indicator of the relationship between individuals.[77] Nevertheless, discipline is maintained and younger corrections officers are able to counsel as well as direct older prisoners.

As might be expected, a substantial number of prisoners (27.5 percent in 1983) are members of *bōryokudan* (ibid.: 71), which presents special problems for prison officials. *Bōryokudan* resist all attempts at rehabilitation, try to intimidate other prisoners and correctional officers, and frequently offer bribes to officers to obtain prohibited materials. Their status as prisoners increases their prestige among fellow gang members. Because the gang takes care of a *bōryokudan* member's family and most return to a higher status job once released, prison is no deterrent, nor does it rehabilitate most gang members. Recidivism among *bōryokudan* members is much higher than that of the general prisoner population, exceeding 70 percent (ibid.). Another *bōryokudan*-related problem facing corrections officials is the increased number of female prisoners who are stimulant drug abusers. As may be seen in table 7.3, the largest percentage of prisoners admitted in 1987 was stimulant drug offenders, an offense that accounted for 55 percent of all female prison admissions. These female offenders also tend to resist efforts at rehabilitation, seeing the offense as a "crime without a victim," and therefore not morally wrong (ibid.: 73).

RECIDIVISM

Recidivism is a problem in any system, but perhaps even more so in the Japanese system because it accounts for such a high percentage of crime. Recidivism is defined in Article 56 of the Penal Code as pertaining to any person who has been sentenced to imprisonment at forced labor and who commits a crime within five years of the date on which the execution of the former sentence was completed. Despite substantial efforts to reduce recidivism, the rate of returning prisoners has remained at about 21 percent for the last ten years; ex-convicts (those who have been previously sentenced to imprisonment or fine) have constituted approximately 64 percent of all prisoners (*White Paper on Crime 1988:* 23). The percentage of prisoners who have committed six or more crimes was over 15 percent in 1988, showing a slight increase over the ten-year period (ibid.: 24). The offenses most frequently committed by multiple-offenders are larceny, bodily injury, and assault, closely followed by fraud and stimulant drug offenses (ibid.: 27), thus showing no pattern with respect to the object of the offense. Sentences by judges for subsequent offenses are little different regardless of how many previous offenses the offender had at the time of sentencing (ibid.: 30). Table 7.4 provides data on various characteristics of multiple-offenders. Most notable is the fact that 60.1 percent of this group had an IQ of 69 or less but that almost 83 percent were diagnosed as having no mental problems and almost 86 percent were junior high school graduates. Only 7.7 percent of the multiple-offenders are *bōryokudan* members, but of that number 17.5 percent are heads of their gangs and 42.4 percent are high-ranking officials (ibid.: 36-37). The low percentage of gangsters among the multiple-offenders is likely accounted for by the

Table 7.3
Percentage of Newly Admitted Prisoners, by Offense (1985-1987)

Offence	1985	1986	1987 Total	1987 Male	1987 Female
Total	100.0	100.0	100.0(29,726)	100.0(28,454)	100.0(1,272)
Penal Code offences	63.0	61.3	62.3(18,518)	63.2(17,996)	41.0 (522)
Homicide	2.4	2.4	2.5 (749)	2.4 (681)	5.3 (68)
Robbery	2.0	1.8	2.1 (614)	2.1 (609)	0.4 (5)
Bodily injury	6.9	6.3	6.7 (1,984)	6.9 (1,971)	1.0 (13)
Assault and unlawful assembly with weapons	0.4	0.3	0.3 (90)	0.3 (90)	—
Intimidation	0.2	0.2	0.2 (51)	0.2 (51)	—
Extortion	3.8	3.7	4.1 (1,217)	4.3 (1,213)	0.3 (4)
Larceny	26.9	26.9	26.7 (7,948)	27.0 (7,676)	21.4 (272)
Fraud	7.3	6.7	6.8 (2,009)	6.7 (1,910)	7.8 (99)
Embezzlement	0.9	0.9	0.9 (266)	0.9 (258)	0.6 (8)
Rape	1.4	1.4	1.4 (427)	1.5 (427)	—
Indecent assault	0.4	0.4	0.4 (120)	0.4 (120)	—
Arson	0.9	0.8	0.9 (257)	0.8 (224)	2.6 (33)
House breaking	0.6	0.7	0.7 (195)	0.7 (195)	—
Violent acts	2.2	2.0	1.9 (568)	2.0 (567)	0.1 (1)
Professional negligence	4.6	4.5	4.5 (1,335)	4.7 (1,329)	0.5 (6)
Others	2.3	2.4	2.3 (688)	2.4 (675)	1.0 (13)
Special Law offences	37.0	38.7	37.7(11,208)	36.8(10,458)	59.0 (750)
Narcotics	0.1	0.1	0.1 (35)	0.1 (33)	0.2 (2)
Stimulant drugs	27.1	28.0	27.0 (8,036)	25.8 (7,337)	55.0 (699)
Prostitution	0.4	0.4	0.4 (133)	0.4 (110)	1.8 (23)
Road-traffic violations	6.6	6.8	6.5 (1,919)	6.7 (1,906)	1.0 (13)
Others	2.8	3.5	3.7 (1,085)	3.8 (1,072)	1.0 (13)

Note: Figures in parentheses show actual numbers.

Source: Annual Statistics on Corrections from Government of Japan, Ministry of Justice, Research and Training Institute, "Summary of the White Paper on Crime" (1988), p. 111.

relatively long sentences they are given, reducing the likelihood of multiple offenses. Parole periods of multiple-offenders tend to be quite short: 78.6 percent of recidivists with six or more offenses had parole periods of three months or less, and 90.2 percent of those with ten or more offenses received parole periods of three months or less (ibid.: 37).

Judges and parole boards seem to be quite lenient with multiple-offenders, reflecting either eternal optimism about the likelihood of rehabilitation or disbelief in the deterrent effects of sanctions. Public opinion on this issue in Japan is mixed. In a survey conducted in July 1986,

Table 7.4
Percentage Distribution on Intelligence Quotient, Mental Disturbances,
Level of Education, and Vicious Habits of Multiple-Convicted Prisoners
by Types of Offenses

Type of offence	Total	Larceny	Fraud	Stimulant drugs	Robbery	Bodily injury	Homicide	Arson	Rape and indecent assault	Others
Total	100.0 (2,159)	100.0 (1,289)	100.0 (291)	100.0 (204)	100.0 (62)	100.0 (54)	100.0 (48)	100.0 (33)	100.0 (24)	100.0 (154)
1) Intelligence quotient (I.Q.)										
69 or less	60.1	61.9	62.5	45.1	59.7	53.7	70.8	81.8	70.8	53.2
70 ~ 79	17.9	17.1	19.2	22.5	16.1	18.5	12.5	9.1	8.3	22.1
80 ~ 89	11.0	10.9	7.2	17.2	8.1	11.1	10.4	6.1	8.3	14.3
90 ~ 109	8.5	7.4	7.9	13.7	14.5	16.7	4.2	3.0	12.5	7.8
110 or more	0.7	0.8	0.3	1.0	—	—	—	—	—	1.9
Not known	1.7	1.9	2.7	0.5	1.6	—	2.1	—	—	0.6
2) Mental disturbances										
None	82.8	81.9	85.9	90.7	87.1	79.6	81.3	63.6	66.7	79.9
Mental retardation	8.0	10.8	3.8	0.5	6.5	3.7	4.2	15.2	8.3	4.5
Psychopath	5.0	4.2	4.5	2.9	6.5	9.3	14.6	12.1	8.3	7.8
Neurosis	0.1	0.2	—	0.5	—	—	—	—	—	—
Other disturbances	3.4	2.5	4.8	4.9	—	7.4	—	3.0	8.3	6.5
Not known	0.7	0.5	1.0	0.5	—	—	—	6.1	8.3	1.3
3) Level of education										
Elementary school	29.9	31.7	22.7	26.5	25.8	20.4	56.3	45.5	29.2	26.6
Junior-high school	55.7	54.4	58.8	56.4	62.9	72.2	37.5	51.5	50.0	58.4
Senior-high school	11.6	10.6	15.5	15.7	9.7	7.4	2.1	3.0	16.7	13.0
College or university	1.5	1.8	2.4	0.5	—	—	2.1	—	—	0.6
Not known	1.3	1.6	0.7	1.0	1.6	—	2.1	—	4.2	1.3
4) Vicious habits										
Alcoholism	22.8	17.5	48.5	—	25.8	42.6	35.4	18.2	29.2	37.7
Drug addiction	10.1	2.6	1.0	76.5	8.1	13.0	2.1	3.0	—	7.1
Gambling	7.7	10.8	2.7	1.0	8.1	3.7	4.2	3.0	8.3	3.2
None	51.2	60.0	41.6	19.1	51.6	35.2	52.1	51.5	50.0	43.5
Not known	8.2	9.2	6.2	3.4	6.5	5.6	6.3	24.2	12.5	8.4

Note: Figures in parentheses show actual numbers.

Source: Government of Japan, Ministry of Justice, Research and Training Institute, "Summary
of the White Paper on Crime" (1988), p. 32.

37 percent of the citizens polled thought that longer imprisonment was
appropriate for multiple-offenders while 38 percent thought that guidance
after release was preferable. Prisoners themselves responded to the survey
with results of 29.1 percent and 33.2 percent respectively (*White Paper on
Crime 1987:* 22). The public also thought that, the *Aizawa* decision (see

chapter 5) notwithstanding, those who kill their parents deserve more severe punishment than other murderers: 33.2 percent were in favor of more severe punishment, 29.9 percent in favor of the same, and 10.1 percent for less severe punishment. Prisoners had even stronger feelings, with 46 percent favoring more severe punishment while 24.1 percent and 13.7 percent favored the same or less severe punishment, respectively (ibid.: 24). Supporting these findings, a substantial plurality of respondents felt that penalties in general were either appropriate (28 percent) or too lenient (18.7 percent), with only 1 percent thinking them too heavy (and 34.6 percent undecided) (ibid.: 26). When asked whether they felt the police and the courts were doing a good job, however, 33.6 percent of the public said they were, while only 18 percent did not think so (and 48.4 percent either did not know or could not give a decisive answer) (ibid.: 25).

When questioned about the corrections system, the public thought that prisons were useful for rehabilitation as well as punishment, by a margin of 36.8 percent to 12.6 percent (with 50.6 percent not knowing or undecided); prisoners themselves agreed, by a margin of 33.3 percent to 21.3 percent to 45.4 percent, respectively (ibid.: 27). A majority (57.8 percent) of the respondents thought that affection in addition to severity is the most effective treatment of prisoners, with only 25.2 percent opting for severity alone; here, prisoners' opinions were more divided, with 80.6 percent agreeing with the severity with affection approach and only 7.1 percent choosing severity alone (ibid.: 28). It is interesting both that prisoners agreed overall with the general public, another illustration of the substantial agreement on societal norms in Japan, and that so many people either did not know or could not give a decisive answer, another reflection on Japanese society. The authors of the White Paper attributed the high percentage of "do not know" and "cannot give a decisive answer" responses to a lack of knowledge of the criminal justice system on the part of the citizens and called for better public information programs (ibid.: 33), but it is also highly likely that the average Japanese citizen is reluctant to criticize the government and its policies and that many of the answers (or lack thereof) reflect this concern.

It is difficult to reconcile the seeming leniency by the judges and parole authority with the fact that only hard-core criminals and those who have committed very serious crimes are sent to prison. As we have seen, a large percentage of offenders are screened out of the system prior to the imposition of any sentence, and therefore it is safe to conclude that those who ultimately are sentenced are the ones who committed the most serious crimes, are the least repentant, or are recidivists. The recidivism rate is high, thus bringing into question the effectiveness of the rehabilitative practices of the corrections system. And yet the system gets generally good marks from the public. No nation has, of course, solved the problem of recidivism or has developed an effective system of rehabilitation, but the impression is that, compared to the other components of the Japanese criminal justice system, corrections is somehow lacking.

PAROLE

Regional parole boards, or District Offenders Rehabilitation Commissions (*Chihō Kōsei Hogo Iinkai*), are located in the eight cities that house high courts, and are responsible not only for deciding on parole and its revocation but for supervising probation offices as well. Parole decisions are made by three-member panels. Article 28 of the Penal Code provides for parole eligibility when a prisoner "evinces genuine reformation" and has served one-third of his sentence, or ten years if sentenced to life. "Reformation" in Japan means more than just good behavior and includes clear manifestations of rehabilitation. Prisoners are classified into four classes based upon the extent to which they have been rehabilitated, with Class Four being the least rehabilitated and Class One the most (Koshi 1970: 101). Classifications are made by prison officials based upon criteria established by the Ministry of Justice in four categories: personal history, including attitude; characteristics of the offense for which imprisoned; nature of the potential parole environment; and miscellaneous matters, including aspects of the crime not considered in the second category as well as whether or not restitution was made. Information on which these evaluations is based is obtained by probation officers and forwarded to the institution in which the prisoner is incarcerated. This information, as well as information from the institution itself, is then used as the basis for placing the prisoner into the appropriate class (ibid.: 101-2). Those in Classes One and Two who have served their minimum term are eligible for parole consideration. If corrections authorities feel that parole is justified, a recommendation is forwarded to the minister of justice, who in turn forwards the case to the appropriate regional parole board.

Decisions by the regional commissions are reviewed by the five-member National Offenders Rehabilitation Commission (*Chūō Kōsei Hogo Iinkai*), which may reverse decisions made by those commissions.[78] If the local commission does not recommend parole, the prisoner may appeal to the national commission (ibid.: 103). The commission granting parole establishes the terms of parole, based on guidelines issued by the Ministry of Justice. The conditions are much the same as found in the United States, and include regularly reporting to a parole officer, maintaining employment, and avoiding those with criminal records. Once parole is approved, there is a brief ceremony at the institution of incarceration. The released prisoner reports to the appropriate probation supervision office, one of which is located in each prefecture (and four in Hokkaido). Parole officers ensure that the terms of parole are followed. They frown on such things as patronizing dance halls and bars, as well as "random association with members of the opposite sex" (ibid.: 104).

Discharged prisoners may apply for "aftercare" assistance, and may be aided by the government if they are having problems reintegrating into society. This assistance may take the form of temporary boarding at a rehabilitation aid hostel (also available to those on probation or parole who are recommended for such treatment), assistance in obtaining employment, meals, clothing, medical care, housing, or other aspects of adjusting to noninstitutional life (Ochiai 1984: 408). Much of the aftercare assistance is provided for by volunteer probation officers and by the private organizations that operate the Rehabilitation Aid Hostels under Ministry of Justice guidelines and subsidization. There are over one hundred such hostels in Japan, caring for an average of ten people each (ibid.: 409). In addition to the hostels and government parole and probation services, there are other private organizations dedicated to assisting convicted offenders, including the Big Brothers and Sisters Association and the Women's Association of Rehabilitation Aid, the latter with a membership of about 220,000 (ibid.).

There is also a rarely used method by which a prisoner may gain freedom, and that is amnesty. Amnesty may be special, when it is granted to a specific person, or general, when it is granted to a large categories of people. Amnesty, provided for in Article 73 of the Constitution, is granted by the cabinet, with general amnesty granted only on special occasions, such as a royal wedding or signing of a peace treaty (Koshi 1970: 106). A general amnesty was granted in February 1989 in honor of the recently-deceased Emperor Hirohito.[79] The amnesty affected about 30,000 people being tried for or having been convicted of various minor offenses, and restored the civil rights of over ten million people who had lost them as a result of convictions for various offenses (*The Japan Times* 2/9/89: 1). The restoration of civil rights was probably more significant than the amnesty given those accused of or convicted of committing minor offenses, due largely to the political implications of restoring the right to vote to such a large number of people.

Any prisoner can request special amnesty (*tokusha*) by submitting an application to the National Offenders Rehabilitation Commission according to procedures outlined in the Amnesty Law. The Commission makes its recommendations through the Ministry of Justice to the Cabinet, which then issues the appropriate amnesty order (Koshi 1970: 106-8).

CONCLUSIONS

The Japanese corrections system enjoys many benefits not enjoyed by the systems of other nations. The highly centralized nature of the system ensures that treatment of prisoners does not vary greatly from one location to the next, that policies are consistent throughout the country, and that expenditures per prisoner are the same. There are a multitude of facilities and programs, thus providing a close match between prison and prisoner, as well as many public and private organizations dedicated to the rehabilitation of offenders. Recidivism is higher than one might expect, but the nature of the offenders sent to prison accounts for much of that. The highly structured and rigid nature of Japanese society at the same time facilitates and makes difficult the integration of the offender into that society. It facilitates integration by making clear the norms and expectations of that society—there are few ambiguities in regard to behavior in Japanese society—and ex-offenders know what is expected of them. This makes it difficult for the nonconformist, however, and many offenders are nonconformists. The *bōryokudan* member is at odds with society in general but abides by the norms of his reference group, his gang, and therefore is caught between competing demands. The average criminal not affiliated with a gang, on the other hand, has no such reference group and may be forced back into criminal activity by the inflexibility of society. On the other hand, the general leniency shown by both the prosecution and the judiciary tends to ensure that only hard-core offenders and those who commit particularly heinous crimes are sent to prison in the first place. As is the case with other institutions of criminal justice in Japan, the corrections system reflects the society as a whole.

8

Crime and Criminal Justice: Conclusions

After having examined the Japanese criminal justice system in some detail, one of the key questions that prompted this examination remains unanswered: why is the crime rate in Japan so low? As is the case with virtually all complex social phenomena, explanations for behavior are tentative, multiple, and time-sensitive. Assuming that we can identify some factors that might explain the low crime rate, another important question arises: are the factors exportable—can they have any effect in another culture? This question will be addressed after we have attempted to seek answers to the first.

An examination of the criminal justice system reveals aspects of the system which could be considered factors in the low crime rate, at least in part, but the criminal justice system cannot be separated from the larger society, making it difficult to determine to what extent each separately is the determining factor. The centralized nature of the system, from police to corrections, clearly results in a high degree of consistency in criminal justice administration. Personnel training is the same regardless of city or prefecture, administrative policies are the same nationwide, and expenditures are based on need, not local tax base. There are, to be sure, variations in interpretations of policy and in the exercise of discretion at all levels, but this is unavoidable and Japan makes a serious attempt to keep such variations to a minimum. Centralization does not necessarily lead to efficiency, particularly if the centralized system is cumbersome. The

Japanese system is not cumbersome, however, although its efficiency tends to be more oriented toward crime control than due process.[80] The rare defendant who contests the charge and finds the case being heard for one or two hours each month may not feel that the system is particularly efficient, but the statistics speak for themselves: clearance rates are above 70 percent and conviction rates above 99 percent. Suspension of prosecution rates are also high (around 17 percent in 1987), but it can be argued that suspension of prosecution is also an efficient means of dealing with certain defendants.

Further examples of efficiency include the high rate of lay participation in the criminal process, ranging from neighborhood watch organizations to volunteer counselors and probation officers. Not only is this an efficient use of money, it is an excellent means of getting citizens involved in the criminal justice process, thereby strengthening the ties between the citizens and the criminal justice professionals. It is also a measure of the degree of consensus on norms and on the role of the citizen in the nation. Technology also adds to the efficiency of the Japanese criminal justice system; Japanese police, in particular, use the latest in technology, whether it be police communications systems or computerized fingerprint identification equipment. The centralized nature of the system lends itself to the use of computers by police and prosecutors, who can keep track of suspects and of criminal records throughout the country with relative ease. For example, a prosecutor contemplating suspension of prosecution can easily use the computer terminal in his or her office to determine whether the defendant has prior arrests and convictions.

The Japanese criminal justice system is prosecution oriented. The prosecutor is granted substantial powers by law as well as tradition, and discretion to match those powers. Lest that discretion be used inconsistently, the Ministry of Justice issues clear and frequent guidelines on its use.[81] Prosecutors exercise substantial control over the police and clearly enjoy a position superior to defense counsel. It should be noted that a great deal of the power of the prosecutor derives not from statutes but from tradition, which accounts for the substantial respect shown the prosecutor by the public and other personnel in the criminal justice system. The prosecutor in Japan, as in most other nations, controls the decision to charge a suspect, and the charge or charges to be filed. But in Japan the prosecutor has substantial control over access of defense counsel to the accused and plays a major role in the sentencing process. A corollary of this power gives the Japanese prosecutor the discretion to suspend prosecution in the interests of justice, even if the suspect has confessed fully to the crime. This suspension of prosecution is a form of unsupervised probation, meaning that the prosecutor in Japan can summarily sentence a person to probation without sending the case to a court of law. This is an example of efficiency, as it diverts significant number of offenders from the criminal justice system, reduces the potential prison population, and results in sanctions without a trial.

Those accused of criminal offenses in Japan do not enjoy the kinds of procedural protections that their counterparts in the United States and some other countries enjoy, despite language in the Japanese Constitution that would seem to provide such protections. This undoubtedly accounts in part for the high conviction rate, which is based to a large extent on the high rate of confessions. Motions to suppress are rarely successful. Trial courts would seem to be highly prone to convict, to rely on the word of the prosecutor, and to rarely question the voluntariness of confessions. Appeals courts, on the other hand, seem to be more likely to question confessions, at least in capital cases.[82] Nevertheless, most cases are not appealed and those that are take many years to be resolved, almost always while the accused is incarcerated. Defense attorneys in Japan simply do not have the tools with which to effectively challenge the prosecutor's allegations, nor is there a tradition of claiming innocence despite one's guilt.

Against this seeming harshness, however, we find many examples of leniency, chief among them the rather high rate of suspension of prosecution, which ranges from slightly over 5 percent in homicide cases to over 44 percent in larceny cases, with an average of 17 percent (*White Paper on Crime 1988:* 95). While critics of this practice may argue that prosecutors are suspending prosecution in cases they could not win in court and thereby imposing a form of probation on those who have not been found guilty, the fact remains that the vast majority of suspensions are in cases where the accused fully confessed. In addition, the suspension of prosecution acts as a sanction only in a limited sense, as there is no form of supervision for those so treated, no record of indictment or conviction, with negative implications coming only when the person is again arrested. My opinion, based on interviews with prosecutors, defense attorneys, and legal scholars, as well as review of numerous cases, is that the primary intent of suspension of prosecution is rehabilitation, and that the "interests of justice," which can hide a multitude of sins in criminal justice systems, in this case truly results in justice.

Large numbers of those who have been convicted have their sentences suspended, many with probation. Probation itself, as well as parole, usually lasts three years or less. Sentences are generally short, especially considering the fact that so many of the defendants and accused have been screened out or diverted prior to the sentencing stage of the process. Prisons in Japan, as in most other industrial societies, attempt a combination of functions, from rehabilitation through isolation to retribution, but judging from the recidivism rate, they are no more successful than most. One cannot, then, look to the Japanese penal system for answers to the low crime rate question.

There are certainly features of the Japanese criminal justice system to which one would attribute the low crime rate, but it is first necessary to take a brief look at Japanese society in general. Although a complete examination would be beyond the scope of this book, there are several aspects of Japanese society that might account not only for the low crime rate but for support of the criminal justice system as well.[83]

Many aspects point to the homogeneity of Japanese society, and of that there can be no doubt. During my residence in Japan there were many occasions when I was the only non-Japanese present, and it was not unusual to go several days without seeing another non-Japanese. While this is not so pronounced in Tokyo or in Okinawa, the former with many foreign business people and the latter with many United States military personnel, it is quite pronounced elsewhere in Japan. Although I was treated quite well, I was clearly an outsider and could never hope to become Japanese. There are relatively small numbers of other Asians in Japan, and while most foreigners cannot distinguish them from Japanese, the Japanese for the most part not only can but do. Foreign residents constituted only .7 percent of the population of Japan as of the end of 1988, with 92.6 percent of them coming from Asia; Koreans accounted for 78.2 percent of the foreign residents of the country (*The Japan Times* 1/27/88: 2). Inasmuch as it is very difficult for a non-Japanese to obtain Japanese citizenship, the vast majority of non-Japanese in Japan are foreign residents. Thus, the outsider stands out, and this hold true not only for the non-Japanese but for the nonconformist Japanese, because the homogeneity of Japanese society extends to behavior as well as ethnicity or race. The Japanese expect foreigners to act differently, but they do not expect fellow Japanese to do so. Nor are they tolerant of deviance. While the normal response to minor forms of deviance is nothing more than a disapproving look, more blatant examples of legal deviance may result in ostracism, social isolation, or even threats and intimidation. This "deviance" may be something as normal in other societies as standing up for one's rights or initiating legal actions as compensation for injuries or other torts (Mouer and Sugimoto 1986: 251).

Norms in Japan are widely accepted, and rigidly and effectively enforced. While some of these norms and their enforcement may seen absurd to the non-Japanese, they clearly have the effect of reducing deviancy and supporting sanctions against it.[84] It also has the effect of reducing individualism, spontaneity, and, to a lesser extent, creativity. One should not get the impression that the Japanese are a cheerless, rigidly controlled, and deviance-free people; there are, to be sure, nonconformists, radicals, and others who do not accept or practice the norms of the majority. And there are opportunities for nonconformity, such as in the bars and clubs frequented by businessmen or Yoyogi Park in the Harajuku section of Tokyo, where wildly-attired young people gather on weekends to dance and generally engage in behavior that would (and does) shock their elders. But even such "nonconformity" is rather strictly controlled as to time and place, and that it happens at all means that it is socially acceptable. Crime, on the other hand, is not acceptable.

Much has been written about the Japanese emphasis on harmony, whether it be in art or interpersonal relationships. A great deal is done to maintain harmony, with the ultimate sanction being the law. As Waga-tsuma and Rosett (1986) put it:

The Japanese cultural assumption . . . is that the various parts of the social organism are hierarchically ordered and in harmony and that those individuals who are not in their place and in harmony with the rest are outside the group. Conversely, those who are outside are a threat to the harmony and order of the group. In such a view, the role of law is to express and reinforce social harmony against external disruptive influences.

Harmony is disturbed by that which is unusual, unexpected, or unfamiliar. Thus, the youths with bizarre apparel and colored hair and faces, dancing to heavy metal music in Yoyogi Park, do not disturb the social harmony because such behavior is allowed, if not expected, there, whereas the burglar or extortionist who goes about his illegal business as quietly as possible does disturb the social harmony because such behavior is not condoned under any circumstances. A teen-ager with a loud "boom box" on a subway or bus would be clearly disturbing the harmony of the conveyance, but would be free to use the device in Yoyogi Park on the weekend without restriction. Although the law could be invoked to enforce the ban against such noise on public transportation, it would be unnecessary, as such behavior is almost unheard of due to the clearly established and strongly held norms against such disturbances of harmony.

Harmony may be upset by individualism, and some scholars have made it a point to compare the relative lack of individualism in Japan to the United States. Perhaps the United States is not an appropriate comparison, as individualism is carried to an extreme there, but it is natural, inasmuch as most of the scholars making such comparisons are from the United States. The discussion of harmony and individualism often takes the form of emphasis on the group orientation of the Japanese. Becker ("Old and New," 1988: 285) said:

One's success was viewed as inextricably intertwined with that of his fellows: one's own failures, whether economic or moral, were viewed as failures of the group. Such views encouraged members of each group to help each other as if members of the same family, lessening the likelihood of crimes committed against any part of the group.

And Vogel (1979: 218) pointed out: "Because an individual in Japan is identified as a member of a group, the group is affected by the reputation of a deviant and therefore exerts considerable pressure on a potential deviant to live up to standards."

Thus, harmony is maintained by the group, which contains the individualism of its members. The vast majority of groups in Japan maintain the same values, with only the *bōryokudan* and the political radicals clearly rejecting these values; variations in values and norms between other groups are relatively minor. Compare this situation to that in the United States, where people identify themselves as individuals first and only secondarily with groups and where groups are frequently poles apart on most major issues. The "pro-choice" groups and the "right to life" groups on the abortion question are examples of this, and there are many more such examples to be found. Americans "stand up for their rights" as individuals more often than as groups, although the intricacies of the legal system frequently require group action rather than individual litigation. Japanese, on the other hand, tend to demand their rights as groups. Clifford (1976: 164) has described the complex relationship between individualism and group orientation by pointing out the effect of individual initiative and drive on upward mobility within the broader group-sanctioned and recognized objectives. Mouer and Sugimoto (1986: 192-94) similarly recognize the individualism of the Japanese as evidenced by the vast number of periodicals available to the people, the great variety of goods available in stores, the subtle differences in the way store owners wrap packages, and the great variety of dress and behavior on trains during non-rush hours. Japanese individualism, then, is quite different from but not less than American individualism.[85] It is, reflecting Japanese culture, more subtle to the foreigner but not to the Japanese. The foreigner might agree that a wide variety of goods is available to the Japanese consumer, but would not detect differences in the way packages are wrapped or the manner in which people's apparel differs. The important point, however, is that Japanese individualism rarely seeks expression in antisocial acts, whereas American individualism frequently does.

The legal culture of Japan is supportive of the crime-control approach to the administration of justice. Becker ("Report from Japan," 1988: 433) cities this approach as an example of the contextualism of Japanese culture, which emphasizes morality over the letter of the law and which rejects the notion of dismissing a case due to a legal technicality when the guilt of the accused is not in question. This is, of course, in sharp contrast to the legal culture of the United States, which places a premium on due process and legal technicalities at the expense of morality. Further examples of this phenomenon are in the Japanese Constitution, which provides protections for the accused very much like the United States Constitution but which in practice means something quite different. One accused of committing a criminal act in Japan is in fact considered guilty and is therefore expected to confess and repent, despite Article 38, Section 3 of the Constitution, which reads: "No person shall be convicted or punished in cases where the only proof against him is his own confession." While this provision requires that evidence other than a confession be presented to the court, it is likely that the quantum of evidence required in addition to a confession would not always be sufficient for a conviction on its own. Society relies on and has faith in the thoroughness of the investigations by the police and the prosecutors to screen out those who are truly not guilty, whereas those elements of the criminal justice system in the United States are not universally trusted by the population.

Mouer and Sugimoto (1986: 263-64) suggest a number of what they call "structural features" in Japan that may account for the low crime rate, features which reflect the culture in general. It may be worth briefly examining some of these features in order to more fully understand how the culture affects the crime rate. The first structural feature they list is the five and one half day school week, which keeps those of school age in the classroom, and therefore not on the streets, longer than those in most other countries. They might well have added the significant amounts of homework assigned students in Japan and the widespread attendance at *juku*, or private tutorial schools. All of this undoubtedly significantly reduces the number of young people who are on the streets at any given time, and therefore should reduce the opportunities for criminal activity, but the increasing rate of juvenile delinquency brings into question how effective this structural feature is likely to be in the future. The key, of course, is that more Japanese youths desire to be in school rather than on the streets, and more Japanese parents exert effective control over their children, both socializing them in the value of education and ensuring that they study longer and harder than in most other countries.

The second feature listed by Mouer and Sugimoto is the large number of people involved in private security. The visitor or new resident in Japan is struck by the extensive use of private security guards, primarily older men in the grey uniform that is common for the profession. They are unarmed, not even carrying a baton or chemical spray, and rarely a walkie-talkie, and therefore do not pose much of a physical deterrent to the determined criminal, but they are a symbolic presence of authority and therefore are rarely challenged. Japanese respect for the aged may also play a factor in their authority role. My impression, however, is that the deterrent effect of these security guards is minimal and that their primary function is service—guiding people to the correct office, parking place, etc., or directing traffic around construction areas—with a significant secondary function of providing employment for those who are retired but still desire to work. Nevertheless, in lieu of empirical verification of Mouer and Sugimoto's thesis, it is possible that the extensive private security industry in Japan accounts to some extent for the low crime rate.

The third feature is the widespread use of security systems for residences and commercial establishments. Although the average residence does not have a security system, other than a dog, perhaps, the average business does. In addition, the Japanese are very careful about locking automobiles and their homes or apartments when they leave them. There seems to be a greater fear of property crimes than crimes against the person, a fear that is based on solid statistics. Again, however, it is difficult to measure the deterrent effect of security systems, although it is probably safe to say that their presence must deter some property crimes. Many homes have barred windows, and apartments frequently have metal doors with peepholes and deadbolt locks. These security precautions illustrate a concern over burglary, whereas the unguarded merchandise in front of stores illustrates an apparent lack of concern over theft.

Another feature listed is the relatively large number of small shops (ibid: 264), a feature that would seem to increase the opportunities for crime. As was described in the first chapter, however, many such small shops routinely leave merchandise on stands in front of their stores unguarded and usually out of view of employees of the shop. It would not occur to the majority of Japanese to steal such merchandise. Literally thousands of students walk past such shops, where audio tapes and other items of interest to the young are displayed on the sidewalk, and seldom is anything taken or do students even jokingly pretend to take anything. Absent empirical evidence, it is difficult to conclude that the large number of small shops has any effect on crime.

Two related features are listed as factors affecting the crime rate: strict gun control and the virtual monopoly on the use of weapons by, as well as the authority of, the police. As we have seen, the vast majority of weapons violations are committed by members of organized crime, and these weapons are rarely used against either citizens or the police but rather on rival gang members. The real issue, however, is whether the lack of access to guns for the average citizen means that fewer crimes will be committed. An article by David Kope in the *American Rifleman* (a publication of the National Rifle Association) makes a persuasive case against the proposition that gun control is responsible for the low crime rate in Japan. Kope attributes the low crime rate to the efficiency and authority of the police, the homogeneity of the society, the internalization of social controls, and tough laws (1988: 28-29, 72-75). There are significant numbers of Japanese who are fascinated by guns, as evidenced by the stores selling very realistic replicas of handguns and assault rifles, the shooting galleries featuring airguns, and the popularity among Japanese tourists of foreign firing ranges using real weapons. But fascination does not necessarily lead to a desire to use a firearm in the commission of a crime, and it is highly likely that strict control of guns reflects the norms of the society in the same way as does the low tolerance of deviance.

A final feature cited by Mouer and Sugimoto is the large numbers of *kōban*, many of which are located by railroad and major subway stations as well as at major intersections. Whether these locations were chosen as a deterrent to crime or as a service to travelers is difficult to say, but many scholars find a relationship between the *kōban* and the low rate of crime. This issue has been discussed in chapter 2, but it is worth further examination, given that it is so widely considered to be a factor in Japan's low crime rate. Vogel (1979: 215), in his discussion of crime control in Japan, notes the effect the *kōban* has on the community: it brings the police officer close to the community and in so doing establishes relationships that are mutually beneficial to the police and citizens alike. But the community must accept the *kōban* and the relationship—it is not something that can be imposed on an unwilling community with the same results, which again brings us back to the central role that culture plays in this equation.

One must also consider the Japanese economy as a factor in the low crime rate, as it has brought relative prosperity to the nation and the vast majority of its citizens. The social stratification one finds in most other industrialized nations is much less in Japan, which has a vast middle class and a very small lower or under class. While Japan has a number of very wealthy citizens, they tend not to practice the opulent lifestyle of their counterparts in the United States and other countries, thereby reducing the perceived disparity between the "haves" and "have nots." In general, then, the vast majority of Japanese citizens are comfortable. They are, however, comfortable under conditions that many Americans would find barely tolerable, as their housing is far from ideal, usually being quite cramped and lacking central heating or air conditioning, both of which are necessary in Japan. Nevertheless, the unemployment rate is very low,[86] the Japanese have both high savings rates and a good deal of disposable income, they tend to drive new cars, and they enjoy (and demand) high quality merchandise and food. To the extent to which crime is related to such economic factors, one can perhaps find some explanation here.

It is virtually impossible to separate the Japanese criminal justice system from Japanese society as a whole in the search for an explanation of low crime rates. The system reflects and is part of the society as a whole. It is equally difficult, if not impossible, to isolate those aspects of the culture which are determinative in the low tolerance of deviance without a great deal more empirical studies of the matter, but it is safe to say that a combination of these variables is largely responsible for the low crime rate in Japan. It is on that note that we turn to the exportability of those elements of Japanese society that are responsible for the low rate of crime.

IMPLICATIONS FOR THE UNITED STATES

One of the reasons that Japanese criminal justice attracts so much world wide attention is because crime is one of the largest social problems in many societies. The drug epidemic in the United States is being called a "war" due to the scope of the problem and the violence associated with it, and many in the United States look longingly at Japan to see if solutions to the problem can be found there. Some scholars think that many aspects of the Japanese approach can be employed in the United States, while others think that much of the success is attributable to cultural factors, and those cannot be instituted elsewhere. Fenwick (1982: 70), for example, lists seven changes that should take place in the United States based on the Japanese experience, ranging from tougher gun control through more efficient law enforcement to better integration of marginal groups into society. Chang (1988: 148) suggests that Americans emulate the social responsibility of the Japanese, while Becker ("Old and New," 1988: 294) argues that Americans can adopt Japanese methods of dispute resolution as a means of reducing crime. Virtually all of the suggestions from scholars who have written on the subject break down into two basic categories: structural changes and cultural changes.

We have noted the efficiency of the Japanese criminal justice system, an efficiency that relies to some extent on the absence of procedural guarantees found in the United States. It also relies on a high degree of centralization. Can the American criminal justice system emulate the Japanese model through structural change and less concern with procedural niceties? The answer is yes and no. The procedural issue rests largely in the hands of the United States Supreme Court for it, like the legislative branch in Japan, is primarily responsible for the law that protects those accused of criminal acts. To what extent the Supreme Court tends toward the due process or the crime control models depends on the justices themselves and to a lesser extent on public opinion. A conservative swing toward crime control started with the Burger court and continued under Chief Justice Rehnquist, but the precedent established under the earlier Warren court remains largely intact. Public opinion may have the effect of nudging the court somewhat more to the right, but the respect for stare decisis remains high. Thus, a pronounced swing toward the crime control model is unlikely even with the great public outcry about drugs and the violence associated with them.[87] A recent call by a panel of distinguished jurists for restrictions on the number of appeals filed by death row inmates, for example, was met by an outcry from civil libertarians who denounced the proposal as a "rush to the gallows." (Greenhouse 1989: A-15). Such changes will not come easily in the United States.

Law enforcement in the United States could certainly be made more efficient through greater centralization and the adoption of national standards. The practice of each town and hamlet in the United States having its own police force is extremely inefficient, but proposals for mergers or regional police forces have generally fallen on deaf ears. Some small towns have contracted out police (and fire) protection to the county—Los Angeles County is a good example—but the practice is anything but widespread. There are also increasing numbers of regional police academies, training potential police officers for a number of different jurisdictions, but these do not readily translate into a single police force. One could argue that independence brings the police closer to the community they serve, but this is also possible with a regional or national police force as well. The United

States could, then, make its law enforcement much more efficient and effective through greater centralization, starting perhaps at the county level and progressing to the state, but the political realities of the issue doom such a move to failure. Law enforcement in the United States is by tradition a local function, and that tradition will not be lost easily.

Prosecution, which is traditionally a county function in the United States, could be made more effective if it were a state function. The vast majority of the laws enforced by the prosecutor are, after all, state laws, and funding variations from county to county could be reduced or eliminated through consolidation. Trial courts in the United States are generally state courts, although there are county and city courts as well. The recruitment of judges varies widely from state to state, ranging from partisan elections to gubernatorial appointment, with virtually no qualifications required other than membership in the bar for a specified period of time. A requirement of specialized training for all prospective judges might well increase the quality, and therefore the effectiveness, of the judiciary, but again tradition and political reality stand in the way. Defense, of course, is much more effective in the United States than in Japan, despite the varying methods by which it is performed, but such effectiveness arguably impedes law enforcement and thus crime control.

While major structural changes such as those suggested above are not likely to take place in the United States, there are some changes to emulate the Japanese system that are feasible, both functionally and politically. One is the application of modern management techniques to law enforcement. This is, of course, already taking place, but the pace is slow. There is no managerial reason why the top officials in law enforcement agencies must have come through the ranks, starting as patrolmen. Lateral entry, such as is found in Japan for mid-level officers, is possible and desirable in the United States as well. Running a law enforcement agency is not much different from running any large bureaucracy, and there is no reason why the requirements for high positions in law enforcement cannot include graduate degrees. If political reality demands that the chief have come up through the ranks, then it should be incumbent on the political entity served by the agency to provide the managerial training necessary to run the agency.

Another Japanese practice that could be adopted without a great deal of debate is the elimination of politics in law enforcement. This would include the appointment or election of police chiefs, which could be replaced by a civil service process or the forwarding of top choices from a panel of experts to a police commission. The Japanese seem to have effectively eliminated the more overt forms of politics from law enforcement, and one can argue that this has increased their effectiveness as a result. Police chiefs should not take their orders from any political party, body, or individual, and funding should not depend on political alliances. Although this issue would not sit well with incumbent politicians, even they realize that they will not always be incumbents, and that political use of the police can work against them just as easily as it can work for them. Community movements to bring about the divorce of politics from law enforcement are likely to be successful, given enough support and patience.

Most of the suggestions above, whether politically feasible or not, have been made before. Scholars and practitioners have long recognized the weaknesses of American law enforcement without ever having studied the Japanese system. That these recommended practices exist and work well in Japan simply reinforces the recommendations. Major changes, however, will not come until there are major changes in the society as a whole, until American society is more like Japanese society. American society will never be as homogeneous as Japanese society, and Japanese society will never be as heterogeneous as American society, thus the effect of homogeneity/heterogeneity on crime will probably never be known. Nor will American society likely adopt most of the norms commonly held in Japan. But American society can become much less tolerant of deviance than it now is, at some cost, of course, to individualism. The Japanese may seem rigid and intolerant to the outsider, but this is in reality a reflection of their great respect for harmony and for the law. They also appear to have a great deal of freedom. While they may not have the freedom to express their individualism wherever and whenever they please, they do have the freedom to walk the streets at any time of the day or night, to openly display merchandise with little fear of theft, and to live without the constant fear of being victimized by crime. Americans may have to make the same choice. It will not be an easy one.

Notes

1. Prior to the reformations brought about by the new code, the prosecutors sat beside the judge's bench in the courtroom, above the defendant and the spectators. They now sit below the bench on the same level as the defense and spectators (Oppler 1977: 25).

2. Virtually all traffic offenses are covered in the national law; local offenses might include parking violations and minor non-moving offenses.

3. The "sexual" crimes likely refer to drunken Japanese businessmen fondling foreign women, a practice that is clearly not socially acceptable but that rarely results in an arrest. Japanese women are also victims of this offensive behavior and generally deal with the situation short of reporting it to the police.

4. Killing one's child or children and then committing suicide is called "oyakoshinjū." It is far more disgraceful to kill one's self and leave the children without a parent than to engage in oyakoshinjū.

5. Contrast this figure with the 10,556 people in the United States killed by firearms in 1987 (FBI Uniform Crime Reports figure). The population of Japan is roughly one-half that of the United States.

6. There is some evidence that bōryokudan violence may be on the increase again, especially in Tokyo. See The Sunday Star-Bulletin and Advertiser 10/15/89: A-31.

7. Infanticides, almost always accompanied by suicide, are not always reported, at least at the national level, because these offenses are not considered extraordinary.

8. "Bullying" (ijime) is defined as inflicting pain "on a specific person or persons repeatedly with physical attacks or such psychological pressure as threat, harassment, ignoring, etc." (White Paper on Police 1987: 72).

9. *Sekigun,* in Japanese; a radical group tied to various international terrorist acts.

10. See Gwen Nettler, *Explaining Crime,* 2nd ed. (New York: 1978), pp. 157-59, for a summary of research on the subject.

11. Figures for 1988 and the first part of 1989 indicate an upward trend, with 1988 registering 63,300 more crimes of a serious nature than the year before (*The Sunday Star-Bulletin and Advertiser* 10/15/89: A-31).

12. It is interesting to note that one type of crime is on the increase in Japan, and that is crime committed by foreigners. Such crimes were up over 50 percent in the first half of 1988 compared to the same period the previous year. Most of the offenders are illegal foreign workers, and prostitution is one of the more prevalent crimes among this group. The National Police Agency has established a Foreign Workers Problem Countermeasure Office to cope with this problem (*The Japan Times* 9/5/88: 2).

13. David H. Bayley's *Forces of Order: Police Behavior in Japan and the United States* was the first major work in English to provide a comprehensive look at Japanese law enforcement. Published in 1976, the work is insightful and pioneering. Five years later Walter L. Ames wrote *Police and Community in Japan,* significant for its coverage of the *kōban* and *chūzaisho* as well as its excellent chapter on organized crime. *The Japanese Police System Today: An American Perspective,* by L. Craig Parker, Jr., was published in 1984, and focuses on how police deal with the problems facing them in modern Japanese society. There are also many articles of varying quality about Japanese law enforcement, most of them in law enforcement journals.

14. Technically, Japan is divided into forty-three prefectures (*ken*), two urban prefectures (*fu*—Kyoto and Osaka), one district (*dō*—Hokkaido), and one metropolitan district (*to*—Tokyo). For purposes of jurisdiction, all subdivisions other than Tokyo will be referred to as prefectures.

15. Tokyo has a Metropolitan Police Department while all other areas have prefectural police departments. The head of the Metropolitan Police Department is a superintendent general (*keishin sokan*), appointed by the National Public Safety Commission with the approval of the prime minister and the "consent" of the Public Safety Commission, while the heads of the prefectural commmissions are chiefs, or superintendent supervisors (*keishi kan*) (Schembri 1985: 40; Police Law, Articles 47-49).

16. Those who enter as assistant inspectors advance to the rank of superintendent in a little over three years, whereas advancement to that rank by entry level personnel takes twenty-five years (Ames 1981: 184).

17. These figures are reported by Walter Ames for the Okayama police school, and are representative for the country as a whole. See Ames (1981: 170-71) for a detailed breakdown of the curriculum at the Okayama police school.

18. Career women are rare in Japan. Women are expected to get married by the age of twenty-five and have children shortly thereafter, devoting their time to caring for their husband and children. Although there is an emerging feminist movement in Japan, it lacks political power. The vast majority of women in Japan not only accept the norms referred to above but actively enforce them. Men are expected to be married by their late twenties, but such expectations on the part of men have little effect on their careers.

19. This city of 514,000 is located 130 miles southwest of Tokyo on the coast in Shizuoka prefecture.

20. Pachinko is a type of vertical pinball that is very popular in Japan. The payoff to winners consists of the steel balls with which the game is played, which are then traded for various prizes. In practice, however, the prizes are subsequently traded for cash in a nearby, and supposedly secret, location. It is illegal to give cash prizes in Japan, but the subterfuge is well known and the law rarely enforced. Pachinko parlors are also notorious for reporting only a percentage of their income for tax purposes.

21. The rate of fatal accidents per 100,000 population was 8.0 in 1983, declining to 7.6 in 1987; the rate per 10,000 motor vehicles declined from 1.5 in 1983 to 1.3 in 1987. The rate of injuries, however, has been increasing slightly over the years (*White Paper on Crime 1988:* 78). It is difficult to compare the Japanese figures with United States figures, because different measures are used in each country, but the United States suffered 48,700 deaths and 1,800,000 disabling injuries in 1987 in a population approximately twice that of Japan (Hoffman 1988: 809).

22. The defendants were being tried for setting fires at a railway station to protest the privatization of the national railways.

23. In late 1988 the JCP official whose telephone was tapped sued the central government, the prefectural government, and the four police officers involved for 33 million yen, saying he suffered mental anguish and that his privacy and freedom of belief had been violated. An inquest of prosecution (see chapter 4) found that the failure to indict was unreasonable (*The Japan Times* 9/6/88: 2).

24. In 1989, Osaka prosecutors quashed the indictment of a former police officer who had embezzled 150,000 yen turned in to the police station as lost property, saying that his arrest, dismissal from the force, and resulting public criticism was sufficient punishment. The prosecutor cited the small amount of money involved and the fact that the former officer's service had been exemplary until the incident in question as mitigating factors. The officer made restitution as well (*The Japan Times* 4/8/89: 2).

25. High police officials take their jobs very seriously. In 1985 a police superintendent committed suicide by pouring kerosene over himself and igniting it. While it was never determined why he committed suicide, many felt it was because his subordinates had failed an opportunity to arrest suspects in the infamous candy-poisoning extortion cases (*The Japan Times* 8/12/85): 6-7.

26. Dollar equivalents will not be given to figures expressed in yen in this book due to the constantly shifting exchange rate. Many newspapers give the rate of exchange for that day. At the time of this writing, the dollar was worth approximately 142 yen.

27. Students in Japan begin studying medicine after two years of general education courses, with the total time to complete basic college/medical school being six years.

28. The police reports play an especially important role in a case because they are considered evidence. Police officers are rarely called upon to testify in court, as their reports are introduced into evidence and become an important element of the government's case.

29. The high school completion rate in Japan is 90 percent, compared to a rate of 73 percent in the United States (*Education Week* 1985: 28).

30. The Japanese woman is expected to marry before age twenty-five, have children immediately, and thereafter devote most of her time to caring for her

children, husband, and household. Mothers frequently take courses in how to tutor their children. The tutoring includes not only helping the child with homework but also bringing food and drink to the studying child. This role of the woman is almost universally accepted in Japan.

31. *Kensatsuchō* is variously translated as "public prosecutor's office" or "public procurator's office," and *"kenji"* is variously translated as "prosecutor" or "procurator." "Prosecutor" will be used in this book.

32. This is true almost without exception in Japanese society, including higher education. It is almost unheard of for one person to be promoted over another chronologically senior, regardless of performance. See Nakane 1970: Chap. 2.

33. Transfers are a common feature of Japanese society, whether in government or private industry. Employees of large firms and of the government are normally transferred every several years, often having to move relatively long distances. These transfers create considerable strain within families; for families with young children it usually means that the father is separated from the rest of the family for long periods of time, as parents do not want to take children out of the school they are currently attending. My neighbor for several months in Japan was a middle-aged man who had been transferred to Nagoya from Tokyo. He tried to visit his family every weekend, a trip which took two hours each way on the *shinkansen* ("bullet train").

34. There has been academic dialogue over whether in fact this is true. See Goodman (1986) and Foote (1986). Suffice it to say that if plea bargaining exists in Japan it is in no way similar to the same process in the United States.

35. I am using thickness rather than number of pages here because most police reports are hand-written using *kanji* (Chinese characters that express a word or idea) and *kana* (Japanese syllabic characters) as well as many photographs and drawings, and are therefore not directly comparable to English-language police reports. Having read many (and written not a few) police reports myself, I can attest to the fact that Japanese police reports are considerably more comprehensive than United States police reports, all else being equal.

36. Article 223 of the Code of Criminal Procedure allows the prosecutor to ask anybody other than the suspect to appear for questioning.

37. Estimates by various prosecutors range from 85 percent to 95 percent of all cases; no hard data are available on this nationwide.

38. Cases referred to family court were those involving juveniles. Under the Juvenile Law of 1948 (*Shōnen Hō*), all people under the age of twenty come under the jurisdiction of the family court, and the prosecutor must refer such persons to this court. The family court may dispose of the case itself or, if it deems punishment appropriate, the juvenile is over sixteen years of age, and the offense is punishable by imprisonment, it may refer the case back to the prosecutor (Dando 1970: 522-23). These latter cases are not distinguished in the overall figures of prosecution and nonprosecution.

39. The other dispositions were: formal trial—4.7 percent; summary proceedings— 61.1 percent; nonprosecution for other reasons—2 percent; and referral to family courts—18.8 percent.

40. Goodman (1986: 45-46) has suggested that suspension of prosecution could be used as a sanction when the prosecutor does not have enough evidence to convict,

that superiors may be critical of a prosecutor who declines to prosecute for insufficient evidence (feeling that the prosecutor did not expend enough effort in gathering evidence), and that suspension of prosecution could be used as a sanction when evidence that is critical to a case was illegally obtained. While this is all possible, there is no evidence to indicate that it in fact takes place. It should also be remembered that the vast majority of cases come to the prosecutor with a confession already obtained by the police.

41. "Traffic Professional Negligence" cases constitute a large percentage of all penal code offenses. These offenses involve causing serious injury or death through operation of a motor vehicle, such operation being considered under Japanese law "conduct of [a] profession" (Penal Code, Article 211). They are similar to negligent or vehicular homicide in the United States, but include any profession or occupation. The penalty is a fine or imprisonment for a maximum of five years, but a high percentage result in suspension of prosecution.

42. 1,000 yen is a very small sum—approximately $7 at the time of this writing—and hardly a sufficient fine for such an offense. This is a result of the failure to change the Penal Code in accordance with changes in the economy. However, judges may impose far more severe fines despite the seeming restrictions of the Penal Code.

43. For an excellent discussion of the *shimatsusho*, see Wagatsuma and Rosett 1986: 488-92.

44. Except in Tokyo, where there are three.

45. See Mayer (1984: 118-20), for the story of a rape case where the defense attorney performed all of the functions described in the preceding paragraph, resulting in suspension of prosecution.

46. See George, "The 'Right of Silence' in Japanese Law," in Henderson, ed., *The Constitution of Japan: Its First Twenty Years, 1947-67* (Seattle & London: University of Washington Press, 1968), pp. 257-77.

47. There is no guilty plea as such in Japan; a defendant who admits his or her guilt has the right to an adversary hearing, a right that can be effectively waived only by agreeing to summary procedures.

48. See the hypothetical criminal offense committed by a foreigner in Koshi (1970: 17-39). Although in this story the accused visited the family of the deceased victim (of an automobile/bicycle accident) at the urging of a Japanese colleague, the accused's lawyer commended his client for taking the action so promptly and explained the cultural context of this procedure (pp. 21-23).

49. A translation of the 1950 case, which does not include the name of the appellant, may be found in Maki (1964: 219-27); the Kojima case translation may be found in Itoh and Beer (1978: 154-57).

50. Both the Abe and Kojima cases may be found in Itoh and Beer (1978: 167-68 and 157-61, respectively).

51. Despite the decision finding Article 200 of the Penal Code unconstitutional, the article remains unchanged in the Penal Code to this day, due to the fact that the Diet has yet to delete or modify the article. The practical significance of this is minimal, as prosecutors abide by the decision and therefore do not charge under that article.

52. The Japanese courts have interpreted the provisions in question in a manner

consistent with their culture and tradition. In addition, the seeming ambiguity is not disturbing to the Japanese, who not only accept but frequently embrace ambiguity. (Wagatsuma 1984: 377).

53. There is one district and one family court per prefecture except in Hokkaido, which is divided into four judicial districts and therefore has four of each.

54. Civil appeals from summary courts must first go to the district court and then to the high court, while criminal appeals go directly to the high court.

55. Such an appeal may be made by either prosecution or defense.

56. The case was initially heard by two judges consecutively (the first was transferred and the second took over his cases) after which time the case was transferred to a three-judge court.

57. Araki (1985: 622-23) suggests that judges may have difficulty shifting from their normal role of endorsing the prosecution's case to that of impartial fact-finder. It is misleading, however, to suggest that the normal role of the judge is to endorse the prosecutor simply because most defendants whose prosecution has not been suspended in effect plead guilty, and as a result the judge relies heavily on the prosecution's case in approving that plea and passing sentence. The judge's role remains that of an impartial fact-finder regardless of what function he is performing.

58. Haruo Abe (1963: 327-31) and Nagashima (1963: 319-21) suggest that the lack of separation between fact-finding and sentencing may cause problems for both the judge and the prosecutor, because evidence about the defendant's character may affect the fact-finding process (and may be hearsay as well).

59. A judgment of acquittal is made when a final judgment has already been rendered, when the punishment has been abolished by law subsequent to the commission of the offense, when a general amnesty has been proclaimed, or when the statute of limitations has run out (CCP, Article 337).

60. Dismissal takes place when the court has no jurisdiction over the accused, where a prosecution has been instituted in violation of Article 340 of the Code (which prohibits prosecution after dismissal without new evidence), where two prosecutions of the same case have been initiated in the same court, or where prosecution is in violation of rules of procedure (CCP, Article 338).

61. One might find it unusual that the minimum term for robbery is greater than the minimum term for homicide. In Japan there are no separate degrees of homicide; causing death through bodily injury or through negligence come under separate sections of the Penal Code (Articles 205 and 210, resp.). In addition, there are more likely to be mitigating circumstances in homicides than in robberies.

62. Suspended sentence (shikkō yūyo) should be distinguished from stay of execution of sentence (kei no shikkō teishi). The former is done by the judge as a form of leniency, the latter by the prosecutor or the Ministry of Justice in cases of insanity, illness, pregnancy, or family dependency, for example (Articles 479-482).

63. Although the death penalty cannot be imposed for ordinary robbery (Penal Code, Article 236), it may be imposed for violation of Article 240 of the Penal Code, "Death or Wounding through Robbery," and for violation of Article 242, "Rape in the Course of Robbery; Death Resulting therefrom." Both of these offenses are considered robbery.

64. Haruo Abe (1963: 335-36) attributes this to Japanese cultural attitudes that were shaped in part by the poor living conditions facing them until relatively recently where, as Abe puts it, "the common people were quick to learn the lesson

that a grain of rice is sometimes more valuable than human dignity" (p. 336). It is also a function, he points out, of a general tendency of judges to be more lenient than the general population due in part to the fact that they are intimately familiar with the causes of crime and the nature of criminals.

65. "Two-inch" refers to the length of the barrel of the revolver. A two-inch revolver is generally the shortest, and therefore most concealable, of the .38 caliber weapons.

66. This is especially true, of course, in a civil law country such as Japan, where a high court decision will only affect inferior courts within the high court's geographical jurisdiction and then only in the instant case, at least in theory.

67. The United States Constitution did not explicity provide for judicial review. The Supreme Court assumed that power in the case of *Marbury* v. *Madison* in 1803.

68. Only fourteen justices took part in the case, one justice being absent.

69. Danelski analyzed divided grand bench decisions between 1950 and 1960, studying a total of 127 decisions and 1,684 votes cast by twenty-seven justices.

70. The Socialist Party was in power in Japan in the immediate post-war period, and appointed the initial fifteen justices (Itoh 1988: 213). Fourteen of these justices took part in the decisions analyzed by Danelski, five of them for the entire period of the study.

71. Dator sent questionnaires to all Supreme Court justices and to 193 high court judges, asking the respondents to indicate agreement or disagreement with twenty-four sentences taken from Hans Eysenck's list of forty. He received eighty usable responses, virtually all from high court judges, and reported both demographic information and responses to the sentences in an effort to determine judge's attitudes as well as the relationship between those attitudes and their personal characteristics. Among other interesting findings, he found that 56 percent of the respondents graduated from Tokyo University, 14 percent from Kyoto University, and 20 percent from prestigious private universities (p. 414). Fifty percent of the respondents thought the treatment of criminals was too harsh, while the other 50 percent disagreed; 40 percent were in favor of eliminating the death penalty (p. 427).

72. When a person is found guilty in Japan the judge must impose a sentence. He may, however, under Articles 25 and 25-2 of the Penal Code, suspend execution of that sentence for certain offenders for a period of from one to five years and may place the offender on probation for the same period.

73. Probation offices supervise both probationers and parolees.

74. These qualifications are not based on education as much as upon standing in the community, stability, and good health (Ochiai 1984: 408).

75. Psychological tests such as the Rorschach inkblot test, thematic apperception test, and sentence completion test, are used extensively in classification institutions (Nomura 1987: 10).

76. Haruo Abe (1963: 356) suggests that the juvenile correctional system is characterized by "excessive idealism and overprotectionism": "Although an idealistic attitude is perhaps necessary to some degree in the administration of criminal justice, sentimental idealism is intolerable when it overwhelms reality." This is particularly evident in the 1951 law that extended the age limit for treatment as a juvenile from 18 to 20; although he agrees in principle with the move, he thinks that it must be accompanied by much better casework. Abe clearly represents one school of Japanese criminology, but he wrote his critique over twenty-five years ago, and

much has changed since then, even though the basic philosophy guiding the system has not.

77. Sex is perhaps more important than age in defining relationships, but in Japan women are rarely in positions of administrative seniority over men, and when administrative hierarchy is not a factor, the younger male is almost always superior to the older female.

78. Members are appointed by the minister of justice with the approval of the Diet.

79. Hirohito's official title after his death is Emperor Showa, after the name of the era that began with his becoming emperor in 1926. The current era under Emperor Akihito is Heisei, and Akihito will be known as Emperor Heisei after his death.

80. See Herbert L. Packer, *The Limits of the Criminal Sanction* (Stanford, Calif.: Stanford University Press, 1968), especially Part II, pp. 149-246.

81. This would lead one to question whether in fact the prosecutor in Japan has much discretion, since discretion granted by law is tightly controlled by rules and guidelines that have the effect of policy. The answer is that the individual prosecutor has only as much discretion as the supreme prosecutor allows, but that prosecution as a system in Japan enjoys considerable discretion.

82. In a 1989 case, the Supreme Court of Japan reversed the death sentence of a man convicted of the 1972 murder of a cab driver. The defendant was convicted on the basis of the confession of an alleged accomplice, which the Court said was highly questionable. The trial court death sentence was upheld in 1982 by the Nagoya High Court, which the Supreme Court criticized for misinterpreting the facts and making erroneous judgments on evidence. This case was the sixth reversal of a death sentence since World War II, and illustrates the slow pace of justice in Japan: the accused was arrested two months after the discovery of the body, but it took over two years for the case to be tried and the defendant sentenced, and another seven years before the first appeal was decided, and finally, another seven before the Supreme court rendered a judgment (*The Japan Times* 6/23/89: 2).

83. There are a number of good works on the subject. See, for example, Ezra Vogel's *Japan as Number One*, Chie Nakane's *Japanese Society*, Edwin Reischauer's *The Japanese*, and Mouer and Sugimoto's *Images of Japanese Society*.

84. Some norms, especially those that apply to women, are rigid. There is, for example, the practice of *koromogae*, or change of dress, which dictates when clothing is changed for the season. This applies not only to school uniforms (virtually all public school children in Japan wear uniforms), but to apparel worn by adults as well, particulary women, whose garments change in style, material, and color on specific dates during the year. To forget or ignore the date and wear clothes that the day before would have been acceptable is to risk scorn, even though the heavy wool clothing that is expected to be worn during winter would be quite uncomfortable on a hot day in October.

85. For a discussion of American individualism in contrast to Japanese individualism, see David Kolb, "American Individualism: Does It Exist?" *Nanzan Review of American Studies* 6, pp. 21-46. This article was written primarily for a Japanese audience.

86. Despite the very low rate of unemployment, there are an estimated 100,000 homeless persons in Japan. They are homeless largely by choice, because various welfare programs are available to provide not only shelter but food and medical care

for those not able to afford such necessities. A number of the homeless are well-educated individuals who have had some personal tragedy that led them to their present state or are those who cannot cope with the norms of the workplace (Yates 1989: D-7).

87. A swing toward the right would result in fewer protections for the accused but greater relaxation on gun control, because the right wing in the United States favors tougher treatment of criminals but few restrictions on gun ownership, pointing out once again the great contrast between the United States and Japan.

Bibliography

Abe, Hakaru. "Education of the Legal Profession in Japan." In von Mehren, ed. *Law in Japan: The Legal Order in a Changing Society.* Cambridge: Harvard University Press, 1963, pp. 153-85.

Abe, Haruo. "The Accused and Society: Therapeutic and Preventive Aspects of Criminal Justice in Japan." In von Mehren, ed. *Law in Japan: The Legal Order in a Changing Society.* Cambridge: Harvard University Press, 1963, pp. 324-63.

Allen, Joan Virginia. "The Japanese Judicial System." *San Fernando Valley Law Review* 12 (1984), pp. 1-10.

Allen-Bond, Marc. "Policing Japan." *Law and Order* 32 (May 1984), pp. 46-52.

Ames, Walter L. *Police and Community in Japan.* Berkeley: University of California Press, 1981.

_____. "The Japanese Police: A General Survey." *Police Studies* 2 (Spring 1979), pp. 6-10.

Appleton, Richard B. "Reforms in Japanese Criminal Procedure Under Allied Occupation." *Washington Law Review* (special edition, 1977), pp. 36-65.

Araki, Nobuyoshi. "The Flow of Criminal Cases in the Japanese Criminal Justice System." *Crime and Delinquency* 31 (October 1985), pp. 601-29.

Archambeault, William G., and Charles R. Fenwick. "Differential Effects of Police Organizational Management in a Cultural Context: Comparative Analysis of South Korean, Japanese and American Law Enforcement." *Police Studies* 8 (March 1985), pp. 1-12.

Archer, Dane, and Rosemary Gartner. "Homicide in 110 Nations: the Development of the Comparative Crime Data File." In Shelley, ed. *Readings in Comparative Criminology*. Carbondale: Southern Illinois University Press, 1981, pp. 78-99.

————. *Violence and Crime in Cross-National Perspective*. New Haven: Yale University Press, 1984.

Bayley, David H. *Forces of Order: Police Behavior in Japan and The United States*. Berkeley: University of California Press, 1976.

Becker, Carl B. "Old and New: Japan's Mechanisms for Crime Control and Social Justice." *The Howard Journal of Criminal Justice* 27 (November 1988), pp. 283-96.

————. "Report from Japan: Causes and Controls of Crime in Japan." *Journal of Criminal Justice* 16 (Sept.-Oct. 1988), pp. 425-35.

Beer, Lawrence W. "Japan's Constitutional System and its Judicial Interpretation," *Law in Japan* 17 (1984), pp. 7-41.

————. "Postwar Law on Civil Liberties in Japan." *UCLA Pacific Basin Law Journal* 2 (Spring and Fall 1983), pp. 98

Berezin, Eric Paul. "A Comparative Analysis of the U.S. and Japanese Juvenile Justice Systems." *Juvenile & Family Court Journal* 33 (November 1982), pp. 55-62.

Bolz, Herbert F. "Judicial Review in Japan: The Strategy of Restraint." *Hastings International and Comparative Law Review* 4 (Fall 1980), pp. 88-142.

Boyd, William B. "Education in Japan," *The Wingspread Journal* (Summer 1984), special section (no page numbers).

Bunge, Frederica M., ed. *Japan: A Country Study*. Washington, D.C.: Government Printing Office, 1983.

Chan, Dae H. "Crime and Delinquency Control Strategy in Japan: A Comparative Note." *International Journal of Comparative and Applied Criminal Justice* 12 (Winter 1988), pp. 139-49.

Charle, Suzanne. "The Tokyo Police Academy." *Police Magazine* 2 (July 1979), pp. 49-53.

Clifford, William. *Crime Control in Japan*. Lexington, Mass.: Lexington Books, 1976.

Cooke, Melinda W. "National Security." In Frederica M. Bunge and Donald P. Whitaker, eds. *Japan: A Country Study*. Washington, D.C.: Government Printing Office, 1983. pp. 341-99.

Dando, Shigemitsu. *Japanese Criminal Procedure*. South Hackensack, N.J.: Fred B. Rothman & Co., 1965 (tr. by B.J. George, Jr.).

————. "System of Discretionary Prosecution in Japan." *The American Journal of Comparative Law* 18 (1970), pp. 518-31.

Danelski, David J. "Individualism in Decision-Making in the Supreme Court of Japan." In Glendon Schubert and David J. Danelski, eds. *Comparative Judicial Behavior: Cross-Cultural Studies of Political Decision-Making in the East and West*. New York: Oxford University Press, 1969, pp. 121-56.

Dator, James Allen. "The Life History and Attitudes of Japanese High Court Judges." *Western Political Quarterly* 20 (June 1967), pp. 408-39.

De Vos, George A. *Socialization for Achievement*. Berkeley: University of California Press, 1973.

Durham, W. Cole, Jr. "Comment: The Relationship of Constitution and Tradition." *Southern California Law Review* 53 (January 1980), pp. 645-56.

Euller-Cook, Schura. "Social Harmony and Low Crime Rate." *The Japan Times* (April 22, 1988), p. 16.

Favreau, Kevin T. "Japanese Offender Rehabilitation—A Viable Alternative?" *New England Journal on Criminal and Civil Confinement* 14 (Summer 1988), pp. 331-49.

Fenwick, Charles R. "Crime and Justice in Japan: Implications for the United States," *International Journal of Comparative and Applied Criminal Justice* 6 (Spring 1982), pp. 61-71.

_____. "Culture, Philosophy and Crime: The Japanese Experience." *International Journal of Comparative and Applied Criminal Justice* 9 (Spring 1985), pp. 67-81.

"A Field Guide to the Yakuza." *Harper's Magazine* 272 (March 1986), p. 20.

Foote, Daniel H. "Prosecutorial Discretion in Japan: A Response." *UCLA Pacific Basin Law Journal* 5 (1986), pp. 97-106.

Futaba, Igarashi. "Forced to Confess." In McCormack and Sugimoto, eds. *Democracy in Contemporary Japan*. Armonk, N.Y. and London: M.E. Sharpe, Inc., 1986, pp. 195-214.

George, B. J., Jr. "Discretionary Authority of Public Prosecutors in Japan." *Law in Japan* 17 (1984), pp. 42-72.

_____. "The 'Right of Silence' in Japanese Law." In Henderson, ed. *The Constitution of Japan*. pp. 257-77.

Goodman, Marcia E. "The Exercise and Control of Prosecutorial Discretion in Japan." *UCLA Pacific Basin Law Journal* 5 (1986), pp. 16-95.

Gotoh, Shojiro. "Japan needs jury system." *The Japan Times* (April 2, 1989), p. 20.

Government of Japan: Ministry of Justice. *Criminal Justice in Japan*. Tokyo. 1983.

_____. Ministry of Justice. Research and Training Institute. *Summary of the White Paper on Crime 1987*. Tokyo, 1988.

_____. Ministry of Justice. Research and Training Institute. *Summary of the White Paper on Crime 1988*. Tokyo, 1989.

_____. Ministry of Justice. Supreme Court. *Justice in Japan*. Tokyo, 1988.

_____. National Police Agency. *Japanese Criminal Police*. Tokyo, 1985.

_____. National Police Agency. *White Paper on Police 1987* (excerpt). Tokyo: The Japan Times, 1988.

_____. National Police Agency. *White Paper on Police 1988* (Excerpt). Tokyo: The Japan Times, 1989.

Greenhouse, Linda. "Judicial Panel Urges Limit on Death Row Appeals." *New York Times*. September 22, 1989, p. A-15.

Haley, John O. "Comment: The Implications of Apology." *Law and Society Review* 20 (1984), pp. 499-507.

_____. "Introduction: Legal vs. Social Controls." *Law in Japan* 17 (1984) pp. 1-6.

_____. "Sheathing the Sword of Justice in Japan: An Essay on Law Without Sanctions." *Journal of Japanese Studies* 8 (1982), pp. 265-81.

Hattori, Takaaki. "The Role of the Supreme Court of Japan in the Field of Judicial Administration." *Washington Law Review* 60 (1984), pp. 69-86.

Henderson, Dan Fenno, ed. *The Constitution of Japan: Its First Twenty Years, 1947-67*. Seattle and London: University of Washington Press, 1968.

Hicks, Randolph D., II. "Some Observations on Japanese and American Policing." *Journal of Police and Criminal Psychology* 1 (October 1985), pp. 69-86.

Hirano, Ryuichi. "The Accused and Society: Some Aspects of Japanese Criminal

Law." In von Mehren, ed. *Law in Japan: The Legal Order in a Changing Society* Cambridge: Harvard University Press, 1963, pp. 274-96.

Hoffman, Mark S., ed. *The World Almanac and Book of Facts 1989.* New York: Pharos Books, 1988.

Hoffman, Vincent J. "The Development of Modern Police Agencies in the Republic of Korea and Japan: A Paradox." *Police Studies* 5 (Fall 1982), pp. 3-16.

Itoh, Hiroshi. "The Courts in Japan." In Waltman and Holland, eds. *The Political Role of Law Courts in Modern Democracies.* New York: St. Martin's Press, 1988, pp. 199-215.

Itoh, Hiroshi, and Lawrence Ward Beer. *The Constitutional Case Law of Japan: Selected Supreme Court Decisions, 1961-70.* Seattle and London: University of Washington Press, 1978.

Japan Society, Inc. *Role of Public Prosecutores in Criminal Justice: Prosecutorial Discretion in Japan and the United States* (Public Affairs Series 14). New York: Japan Society, Inc., 1980.

Japan Times. August 12, 1985. "Japanese Police Superintendent Sets Himself on Fire, Dies." pp. 6-7.

————. August 5, 1987. "Police Talked with Negotiators on Penalties for Wire-tappers," p. 3.

————. August 5, 1987. "Prosecutors Let Four Police Off in Wiretapping of JCP Official," p. 2.

————. January 27, 1989. "Number of Foreign Residents Reaches 0.7% of Population," p. 2.

————. September 5, 1988. "Police to Establish Task Force to Deal with Foreigners' Crimes," p. 2.

————. September 6, 1988. "JCP Official Sues for Yen 33 Million in November 1986 Wiretapping Case," p. 2.

————. September 30, 1988. "Chukakuha Group Suspected in Bombing of Judges' Cars," p. 3.

————. February 21, 1989. "Bar Owner Cleared of Raping Girl; Judge Says Evidence Fabricated," p. 2.

————. April 5, 1989. "Ministry Appoints 51 Prosecutors," p. 2.

————. April 8, 1989. "Cop's Indictment Quashed in Alleged Embezzlement," p. 2.

————. June 23, 1989. "1975 Death Sentence is Upset; Supreme Court Orders Retrial," p. 2.

————. June 30, 1989. "Court Nullifies Compensation for Acquitted Murder Suspect," p. 2.

————. August 13, 1989. "Crimes of Our Times," p. 18.

Johnson, Elmer H., ed. *International Handbook of Contemporary Developments in Criminology.* Westport, Conn.: Greenwood Press, 1983.

Johnson, Elmer H., and Hisashi Hasegawa. "Prison Administration in Contemporary Japan: Six Issues." *Journal of Criminal Justice* 15 (1987), pp. 65-74.

Kaiser, Günther. *Prison Systems and Correctional Laws: Europe, the United States and Japan.* Dobbs Ferry, N.Y.: Transnational Publishers, Inc., 1984.

Kawashima, Takeyoshi. "The Status of the Individual in the Notion of Law, Right, and Social Order in Japan." In Charles A. Moore, ed. *The Japanese Mind.* Tokyo: Charles E. Tuttle Co., 1973, pp. 245-61.

Kim, Yongjin. "Work—The Key to the Success of Japanese Law Enforcement." *Police Studies* 10 (Fall 1987), pp. 109-17.

Kolb, David. "American Individualism: Does It Exist?" *Nanzan Review of American Studies* 6 (1984), pp. 21-45.

Kopel, David C. "Japanese Gun Laws and Crime." *American Rifleman*, December 1988, pp. 28-29, 72-75.

Koshi, George M. *The Japanese Legal Advisor: Crimes and Punishments.* Rutland, Vt. and Tokyo: Charles E. Tuttle Co., 1970.

Kumagai, Fumie. "Filial Violence in Japan." *Victomology* 8 (Summer-Fall 1983), pp. 173-94.

Kumasaka, Yorihiko, Robert J. Smith, and Hitoshi Aiba. "Crimes in New York and Tokyo: Sociocultural Perspectives." *Community Mental Health Journal* 11 (1975), pp. 19-26.

Ladbrook, Denis A. "Why Are Crime Rates Higher in Urban than in Rural Areas?—Evidence from Japan." *Australian and New Zealand Journal of Criminology* 21 (June 1988), pp. 81-103.

Lunden, Walter A. "Violent Crimes in Japan in War and Peace, 1933-74." *International Journal of Criminology and Penology* 4 (1976), pp. 349-63.

McCormack, Gavan. "Crime, Confession, and Control." In McCormack, Gavan, and Yoshio Sugimoto, eds. *Democracy in Contemporary Japan.* Armonk, N.Y. and London: M.E. Sharpe, Inc., 1986, pp. 186-94.

McCormack, Gavan, and Yoshio Sugimoto, eds. *Democracy in Contemporary Japan.* Armonk, N.Y. and London: M.E. Sharpe, Inc., 1986.)

McNamara, Joseph D. "Japan's Public Attitude Toward Crime and Law Enforcement Offers a Lesson to the United States." *Security Systems Digest* 12 (June 10, 1981), pp. 8-9.

Mahler, Irwin, Lisa Greenberg, and Haruo Hayashi. "A Comparative Study of Rules of Justice: Japanese versus American." *Psychologia* 24 (1981), pp. 1-8.

Maki, John M. *Court and Constitution in Japan.* Seattle: University of Washington Press, 1964.

Mayer, Cynthia. "Japan: Behind the Myth of Japanese Justice." *The American Lawyer* 6 (July/August 1984), pp. 113-24.

von Mehren, Arthur Taylor, ed. *Law in Japan: The Legal Order in a Changing Society.* Cambridge: Harvard University Press, 1963.

Merriman, David. "Homicide and Deterrence: The Japanese Case." *International Journal of Offender Therapy and Comparative Criminology* 32 (April 1988), pp. 1-16.

Meyers, Howard. "Revisions of the Criminal Code of Japan During the Occupation." *Washington Law Review* (special edition 1977), pp. 66-96.

Mitsui, Makoto. "Kensatsukan no Kisō Yūyo Sairyō."("Prosecutor's Discretion in the Suspension of Prosecution: Historical and Empirical Analysis.") *Hōgaki Kyōkai Zasshi* 91 (1974), pp. 1693-1739.

Miyazawa, Koichi. "Victimological Studies of Sexual Crimes in Japan." *Victimology: An International Journal* 1 (Spring 1976), pp. 107-29.

Mouer, Ross, and Yoshio Sugimoto. *Images of Japanese Society.* London: KPI, 1986.

Murai, Toshikuni. "Current Problems of Juvenile Delinquency in Japan." *Hitotsubashi Journal of Law and Politics* 16 (1988), pp. 1-10.

Nagashima, Atsushi. "The Accused and Society: The Administration of Criminal Justice in Japan." In von Mehren, ed. *Law in Japan: The Legal Order in a Changing Society.* Cambridge: Howard University Press, 1963 pp. 297-23.

Nakane, Chie. *Japanese Society*. Berkeley and Los Angeles: University of California Press, 1970.

Nettler, Gwynn. *Explaining Crime*, 2nd ed. New York: McGraw-Hill, Inc., 1978.

"New Faces of the Sokaiya." *The Economist* 302 (February 21, 1987), p. 70.

Noda, Yosiyuki. *Introduction to Japanese Law*. Tokyo: University of Tokyo Press, 1976 (tr. by Anthony H. Angelo).

Nomura, Yukio. "Recent Trends in the Japanese Prison Service." *Prison Service Journal* 67 (July 1987), pp. 6-9.

Ochiai, Kiyotaka. "Offenders' Rehabilitation in Japan." *New Zealand Law Journal* (December 1984), pp. 407-9.

Ono, Takashi. "Two Amnesties to Cover 11 Million People, February 24," *The Japan Times*, February 9, 1989, p. 1.

Oppler, Alfred C. *Legal Reform in Occupied Japan*. Princeton: Princeton University Press, 1976.

_____. "The Reform of Japan's Legal and Judicial System Under Allied Occupation." *Washington Law Review* (special edition 1977), pp. 1-35.

Parker, L. Craig, Jr. *The Japanese Police System Today: An American Perspective*. Tokyo, New York, and San Francisco: Kodansha International Ltd., 1984.

Parker, Richard B. "Law and Language in Japan and in the United States." *Osaka University Law Review* 34 (March 1987), pp. 47-71.

Peterson, Richard E., and K. K. Seo. "Crime Trends—East and West." *International Journal of Social Economics* 13 (1986), pp. 68-76.

Schoenberger, Karl. "'Bird Cages': Legal Trap for Japanese." *Los Angeles Times*. April 28, 1989, pp. 1, 12-13.

"The Shape of Japanese Schooling: A Statistical Profile." *Education Week* IV February 20, 1985), p. 28.

Schubert, Glendon and David J. Danelski, eds. *Comparative Judicial Behavior: Cross-Cultural Studies of Political Decision-Making in the East and West*. New York: Oxford University Press, 1969, pp. 121-56.

Shelley, Louise I., ed. *Readings in Comparative Criminology*. Carbondale: Southern Illinois University Press, 1981.

Shikita, Minoru. "Law Under the Rising Sun." 20 *The Judges' Journal* 20 (Winter 1981), pp. 42-47.

_____. "Prosecutorial Powers and Discretion in Japan." In Japan Society, Inc., *Role of Public Prosecutors in Criminal Justice: Prosecutorial Discretion in Japan and the United States* (Public Affairs Series 14). New York: Japan Society, Inc., 1980. pp. 5-9.

Suzuki, Yoshio. "Safeguards Against Abuse of Prosecutorial Powers." In Japan Society, Inc., *Role of Public Prosecutors In Criminal Justice: Prosecutorial Discretion in Japan and The United States* (Public Affairs Series 14). New York: Japan Society, Inc., 1980, pp. 13-16.

Takahashi, Sadahiko, and Carl B. Becker. "Organized Crime in Japan." *Organized Crime Digest* 5 (December 1984), pp. 1-5.

Takayanagi, Kenzo. "A Century of Innovation: The Development of Japanese Law, 1868-1961," In von Mehren, ed., *Law in Japan: Legal Order in Changing Society*. Cambridge: Harvard University Press, 1963, pp. 14-40.

Tanaka, Hideo, ed. *The Japanese Legal System*. Tokyo: Univeristy of Tokyo Press, 1984 (rev. ed.) (assisted by Malcolm D. H. Smith).

_____. "The Conflict between Two Legal Traditions in Making the Constitution of Japan." In Ward and Yoshikazu, eds. *Democratizing Japan*. Honolulu: University of Hawaii Press, 1987, pp. 107-32.

_____. "Legal Equality Among Family Members in Japan—The Impact of the Japanese Constitution of 1946 on the Traditional Family System." *Southern California Law Review* 53 (1980), pp. 611-43.

"Thugs Beware." *Time* 131 (March 14, 1988), p. 42.

Toby, Jackson. "Affluence and Adolescent Crime." In Shelley, ed., *Readings in Comparative Criminology*. Carbondale: Southern Illinois University Press, 1981, pp. 18-43.

Tokoro, Kazuhiko. "Japan." In Johnson, ed., *International Handbook of Contemporary Developments in Criminology*. Westport, Conn.: Greenwood Press, 1983, pp. 409-25.

Tokuoka, Hideo, and Albert K. Cohen. "Japanese Society and Delinquency." *International Journal of Comparative and Applied Criminal Justice* 11 (Spring 1987), pp. 13-22.

"Top Japan gang picks leader, plans celebration." *The* (Honolulu) *Sunday Star-Bulletin and Advertiser* (May 21, 1989), p. E-3.

Uctmann, Donald L., Richard P. Blessen, and Vince Maloney. "The Developing Japanese Legal System: Growth and Change in the Modern Era." *Gonzaga Law Review* 23 (1987-88), pp. 349-59.

Ueno, Haruo. "The Japanese Police: Education and Training." *Police Studies* 2 (Spring 1979), pp. 11-17.

United Nations. "United Nations Crime Survey (1977)." In Shelley, ed. *Readings in Comparative Criminology*. Southern Illinois University Press, 1981, pp. 153-74.

Vogel, Ezra F. *Japan as Number One*. Cambridge: Harvard University Press, 1979.

Wagatsuma, Hiroshi. "Some Cultural Assumptions Among the Japanese." *Japan Quarterly* 31 (1984), pp. 371-79.

Wagatsuma, Hiroshi, and Arthur Rosett. "The Implications of Apology: Law and Culture in Japan and the United States." *Law and Society Review* 20 (1986) pp. 461-98.

Wagatsuma, Sakae. "Guarantee of Fundamental Human Rights Under the Japanese Constitution." *Washington Law Review* (special edition 1977), pp. 146-66.

Waltman, Jerold L. and Kenneth M. Holland, eds. *The Political Role of Law Courts in Modern Democracies*. New York: St. Martin's Press, 1988.

Ward, Robert E., and Sakamoto Yoshikazu, eds. *Democratizing Japan: The Allied Occupation*. Honolulu: University of Hawaii Press, 1987.

White, Merry I. "Japanese Education: How Do They Do It?" *Japan Society Newsletter*. September 1984, pp. 2-9.

Wolpin, Kenneth I. "A Time Series-Cross Section Analysis of International Variation in Crime and Punishment." *The Review of Economics and Statistics* 62 (August 1980), pp. 417-23.

Index

About the Author

A. DIDRICK CASTBERG is Professor of Political Science at the University of Hawaii. He has published in the areas of U.S. Constitutional Law, Criminal Justice, and Public Policy.